crocheted animal hats

crocheted animal hats

35 super simple hats to make for babies, kids, and the young at heart

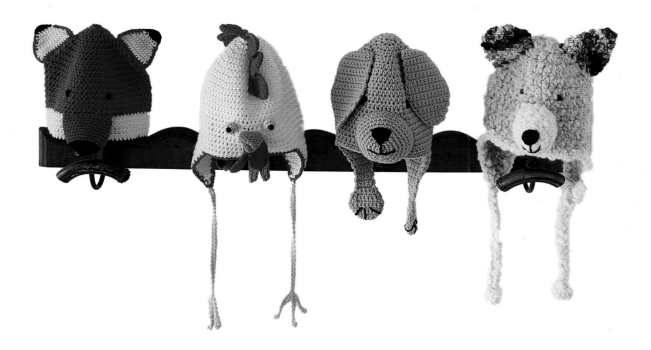

Nicki Trench

CICO BOOKS

LONDON NEW YORK

Published in 2017 by CICO Books
An imprint of Ryland Peters & Small Ltd
341 E 116th St, New York NY 10029

www.rylandpeters.com

10 9 8 7 6 5 4 3 2

Text © Nicki Trench 2017
Design, illustration, and photography
© CICO Books 2017

A CIP catalog record for this book is available
from the Library of Congress.

ISBN: 978 1 78249 428 7

Printed in China

Editor: Marie Clayton
Pattern checker: Jane Czaja
Designer: Alison Fenton
Photographers: Terry Benson and Emma Mitchell
Stylists: Rob Merrett and Sophie Martell
Illustrator: Stephen Dew

In-house editor: Anna Galkina
Art director: Sally Powell
Production manager: Gordana Simakovic
Publishing manager: Penny Craig
Publisher: Cindy Richards

contents

introduction

One of the joys of crochet is in making hats, and you're going to have so much fun creating these quirky and fun ones based on animals. They are quick and relatively easy to make—the skill is in the attention to detail to get the character of each animal. Pricked-up ears or floppy ears, cute little noses… they are all irresistible.

Many of the characters in this book are based on animals that I have owned, or have known in my life, and I have a lot of affection for them. There's Monty, our Border Collie, who lived until he was 18; Poppy the Retriever, who was the smelliest and muddiest dog I've known; and Limoney, my favorite pet Hen. I don't think I know any Grizzly Bears or Tigers personally, but I'm sure there will be someone out there with a tale to tell, who is just chomping at the bit to make these gorgeous hats—and talking of "bits" just look how cute Phoebe the Pony is.

The hats come in three basic sizes: 6–24 months, 3–10 years, and adult. But the basic hat design is similar in most of them, so you can mix and match—if you want to make an animal in a different size to the one in the pattern, simply follow a pattern for your chosen size and add the facial features from the animal of your choice. The same goes for the thickness of yarn—most of these hats are made using worsted weight yarn, but if you want to use light worsted instead, just find one of the patterns made in that thickness for the hat. Then use the instructions from the animal of your choice for the facial details.

I think it's terribly important to think about safety when making hats for children—and even though some patterns are for adult sizes, they may get into the hands of small children because they are so cute. For this reason I have embroidered most of the eyes—if you use safety eyes on just one layer of crochet, there is a risk that they may come loose and become a choking hazard. I haven't used buttons for the same reason, because the thread on the button may come loose. However, I've used safety eyes where the faces have googly eyes and are stuffed, or if they have more than one layer of crochet to cover the back, as they have the added layer of stuffing or crochet fabric to keep them secure.

The hats are made by crocheting in the round (in a spiral), so it's important to use a stitch marker to mark the beginning of each round. I use a small length of contrasting yarn, but you can buy commercial stitch markers that work just as well. It's really important to get the facial details right, so I also used a stitch marker at the bottom of the center front when adding the facial details. This ensures you don't get wonky noses, ears, and mouths… but don't worry too much, as the wonkiness does also give the hats character!

The patterns are suitable for any level of crocheter, you just have to have knowledge of the basic stitches and how to crochet in the round (spirals).

I hope you have as much fun making these characters as I did inventing them. Enjoy.

crochet techniques

Holding your hook and yarn

Holding the yarn and hook correctly is a very important part of crochet and once you have practiced this it will help you to create your stitches at an even gauge.

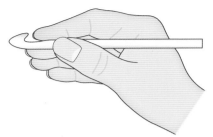

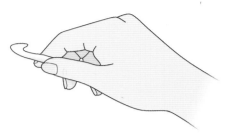

Holding your hook

There are two basic ways of holding the hook. I always teach the pen position as I find this more comfortable. It gives you a more relaxed arm and shoulder.

Pen position Pick up your hook as though you are picking up a pen or pencil. Keeping the hook held loosely between your fingers and thumb, turn the hook so that the tip is facing up and the hook is balanced in your hand and resting in the space between your index finger and your thumb.

Knife position But if I'm using a very large hook and chunky yarn, then I may sometimes change and use the knife position. I crochet a lot and I've learned that it's important to take care not to damage your arm or shoulder by being too tense. Make sure you're always relaxed when crocheting and take breaks.

Holding your yarn

Pick up the yarn with your little finger on the opposite hand to the hook, with palm facing toward you, the short end in front of the finger and the yarn in the crease between little finger and ring finger. Turn your hand to face downward (see right), placing the long yarn strand on top of your index finger, under the other two fingers, and wrapped right around the little finger. Then turn your hand to face you (far right), ready to hold the work in your middle finger and thumb.

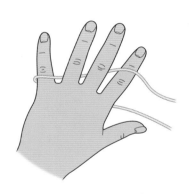

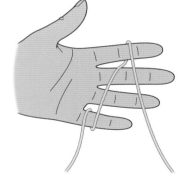

Holding hook, yarn, and crochet

Keep your index finger, with the yarn draped over it, at a slight curve, and hold your work (or the slip knot) using the same hand, between your middle finger and your thumb and just below the crochet hook and loop/s on the hook.

As you draw the loop through the hook release the yarn on the index finger to allow the loop to stay loose on the hook. If you tense your index finger, the yarn will become too tight and pull the loop on the hook too tight for you to draw the yarn through.

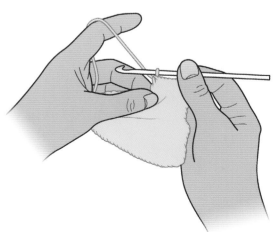

Holding hook, yarn, and crochet for left-handers

Some left-handers learn to crochet like right-handers, but others learn with everything reversed—with the hook in the left hand and the yarn in the right.

Yarn over hook (yoh)

To create a stitch, you'll need to catch the yarn with the hook and pull it through the loop. Holding your yarn and hook correctly, catch the yarn from behind with the hook pointing upward. As you gently pull the yarn through the loop on the hook, turn the hook so that it faces downward and slide the yarn through the loop. The loop on the hook should be kept loose enough for the hook to slide through easily.

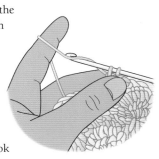

Slip knot

A slip knot is the loop that you put onto the hook to start any stitch in crochet.

1 Make a circle of yarn as shown.

2 In one hand hold the circle at the top where the yarn crosses, and let the tail drop down at the back so that it falls across the center of the loop. With your free hand or the tip of a crochet hook, pull a loop through the circle.

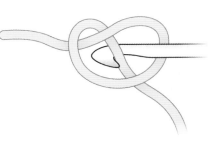

3 This forms a very loose loop on the hook.

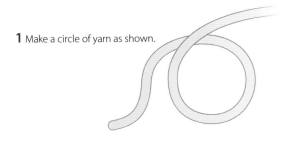

4 Pull both yarn ends gently to tighten the loop around the crochet hook shank.

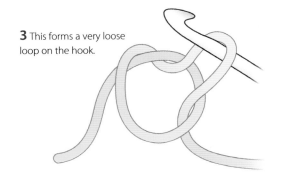

5 Make sure the loop is not TOO tight. It needs to slip easily along the shank.

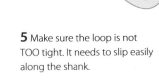

Chain stitches (ch)

Chains are the basis of all crochet. This is the stitch you have to practice first because you need to make a length of chains to be able to make the first row or round of any other stitch. Practicing these will also give you the chance to get used to holding the hook and the yarn correctly.

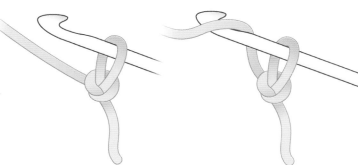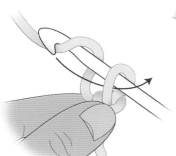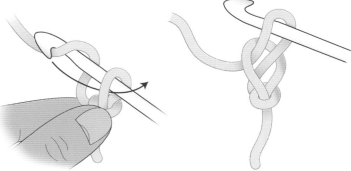

1 Start with the tip of the hook pointed upward, with the slip knot on your hook sitting loosely so there is enough gap to pull a strand of yarn through the loop on the hook.

2 Catch the yarn with the hook, circling it around the strand of yarn.

3 As you catch the yarn, turn the tip of the hook downward, holding the knot immediately under the loop on the hook with your left hand between finger and thumb.

4 Then gently pull the strand of yarn through the loop on the hook. As soon as the tip of the hook comes through the loop, turn the tip of the hook immediately upward.

Making rounds

When working in rounds the work is not turned, so you are always working from one side. Depending on the pattern you are working, a "round" can be square. You may need to make a turning chain to create the height you need for the stitch you are working, as listed under making rows (right). Or, you may work in a spiral, in which case you do not need a turning chain.

To keep count of where you are in the pattern, you will need to place a stitch marker at the beginning of each round; a piece of yarn in a contrasting color is useful for this.

Making rows

When making straight rows you need to make a turning chain to create the height you need for the stitch you are working with, as follows:
Single crochet = 1 chain
Half double crochet = 2 chain
Double crochet = 3 chain
Treble = 4 chain
Double treble = 5 chain
Triple treble = 6 chain

Stitch markers

There are commercial stitch markers available on the market, made of plastic or metal. Some are decorative and have little beads at the end, and the plastic ones can look like little safety pins or hooks. I find using a contrasting piece of yarn a much better option that works for me as I tend to lose the tiny plastic ones down the back of my chair or sofa, but it doesn't matter if you lose a piece of yarn—you can just cut another piece. Cut a piece of yarn about

4in (10cm) long in a contrasting color and loop the strand into the first stitch; when you have made a round and reached the point where the stitch marker is, work this stitch, take out the stitch marker from the previous round and put it back into the first stitch of the new round.

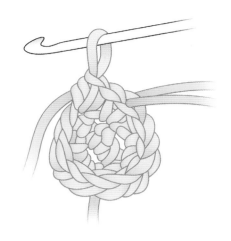

How to measure a gauge square

Make a number of chains that measure to approximately 5–6in (13–15cm) using the hook and the yarn recommended in the pattern. Make enough rows to form a square and then fasten off.

Take a tape measure or ruler, place it across your crocheted piece horizontally, and mark off an area of 4in (10cm) with pin markers. Count the number of stitches across 4in (10cm), then take the tape measure/ruler and place it vertically and count the number of rows across 4in (10cm). Compare the number of stitches and rows you have counted to the gauge guide in the pattern. If your rows and stitches measure the same as the guide, use this size hook and yarn to achieve the same gauge and measurements in the pattern. If you have more stitches, then your gauge is tighter than the sample and you need to use a larger crochet hook, if you have fewer stitches, then your gauge is looser and you'll need to use a smaller hook. Make gauge squares using different size hooks until you have reached the same gauge as the guide and then use this hook to make the project.

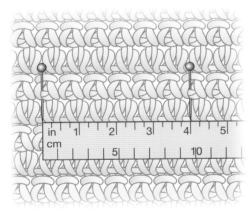

Joining in a new ball of yarn

You may need to join a different ball of yarn when either the ball runs out or you need to bring in a new color. If joining when the ball runs out, try and join at the end of the row.

Joining at the end of a row/round

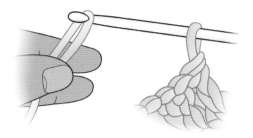 

1 Keep the loop of the old yarn on the hook. Drop the tail and catch a loop of the strand of the new yarn with the crochet hook.

2 Pull the new yarn through the loop on the hook, keeping the old loop drawn tight.

Joining in the middle of a row

Sometimes you will need to join in a new yarn in the middle of the row, either because the yarn has run out and you need to use the same color but with a new ball, or when instructed in the pattern to change color. In this case you work part of the stitch in the old yarn and then switch to the new yarn to complete it, as explained in the instructions for joining on double crochet, below.

How to join in a new yarn on single crochet

Make a single crochet stitch as usual, but do not complete the stitch. When there are two loops remaining on the hook, drop the old yarn, catch the new yarn with the hook and pull it through these two loops to complete the stitch.

Continue to crochet with the new yarn. Cut the strand of the old yarn about 6in (15cm) from the crochet and leave it to drop at the back of the work so you can sew this end in later.

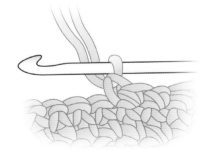 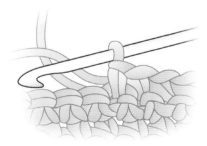

Slip stitch (ss)

A slip stitch is the shortest crochet stitch and is usually worked into other stitches rather than into a foundation chain, because it is rarely used to make a whole piece of crochet. It is mainly used to join rounds or to take the yarn neatly along the tops of stitches to get to a certain point without having to fasten off. It can also be used as to join pieces.

1 To make a slip stitch, first insert the hook through the stitch (chain or chain space). Then wrap the yarn over the hook.

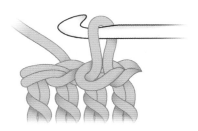

2 Pull the yarn through both the stitch (chain or chain space) and the loop on the hook at the same time, so you will be left with one loop on the hook.

Single crochet (sc)

Single crochet is the most commonly used stitch of all. It makes a firm tight crochet fabric. If you are just starting out, it is the best stitch to start with because it is the easiest to make.

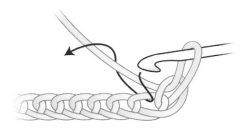

1 Make a foundation chain, then insert the tip of the hook into the 2nd chain from the hook. Catch the yarn with the hook by taking the hook around the back of the yarn strand. Pull the yarn through the chain only, with the hook pointed downward. As soon as you have brought the yarn through, immediately turn the hook upward—this will help to keep the loop on the hook and prevent it sliding off. Keep the hook in a horizontal position.

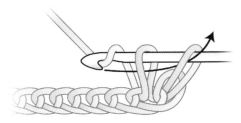

2 You will now have two loops on the hook. Wrap the yarn over the hook again (with the hook sitting at the front of the yarn), turn the hook to face downward and pull the yarn through the two loops, turning the hook to point upward as soon as you have pulled the yarn through.

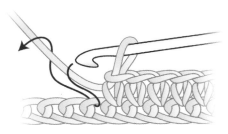

3 One loop is now left on the hook. Keep the hook pointed upward (this is the default position of the hook until you start the next stitch). Continue working one single crochet in each chain to the end of the foundation chain.

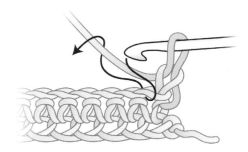

4 Then turn the work to begin the next row. Make one chain and work the first single crochet into the top of the first single crochet in the row below (picking up the two loops at the top of the stitch). Work one single crochet in each single crochet stitch in the row below, to the end of the row.

5 For all subsequent rows, repeat Step 4.

Half double crochet (hdc)

Half double crochet are stitches that are the next height up to a single crochet stitch. The yarn is wrapped over the hook first before going into the stitch (or space), and then once pulled through the stitch (or space) there will be three loops on the hook. The middle loop is from the strand that was wrapped over the hook. Before you attempt to pull the yarn through all three stitches, make sure the loops sit straight and loosely on the hook so that you can pull another strand through to complete the stitch.

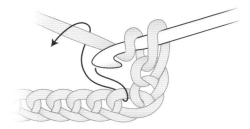

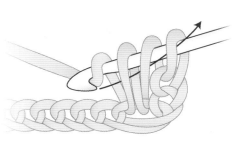

1 Make your foundation chain as usual to start. Before inserting the hook into the work, wrap the yarn over the hook. Then with the yarn wrapped over the hook, insert the hook through the 3rd chain from the hook. Work "yarn over hook" again (as shown by the arrow).

2 Pull the yarn through the chain. You now have three loops on the hook. Yarn over hook again and pull it through all three loops on the hook.

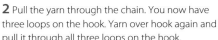

3 You will be left with one loop on the hook. Continue working one half double crochet in each chain to the end of the foundation chain.

4 Then turn the work to begin the next row. Make two chain. Work one half double crochet in each half double crochet stitch in the row below to the end of the row.

5 For all subsequent rows, repeat Step 4.

Double crochet (dc)

A double crochet is a very common stitch; it gives a more open fabric than a single crochet or a half double crochet, which both give a denser fabric, and it's a one step taller stitch than a half double crochet. As with the half double crochet, the yarn is wrapped over the hook first before going into the stitch (or space) and then, once pulled through the stitch, there will be three loops on the hook. The middle loop is from the strand that was wrapped over the hook. Before you attempt to pull the yarn through the next two stitches on the hook, make sure the loops sit straight and loosely on the hook so that you can pull another strand through the loops on the hook.

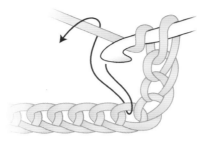

1 Before inserting the hook into the work, wrap the yarn over the hook. Then with the yarn wrapped over the hook, insert the hook through the 4th chain from the hook. Work "yarn over hook" again (as shown by the arrow).

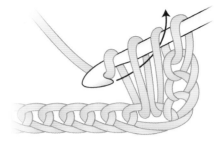

2 Pull the yarn through the chain. You now have three loops on the hook. Yarn over hook again and pull it through the first two loops on the hook.

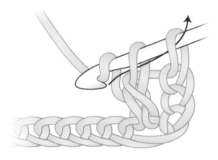

3 You now have two loops on the hook. Yarn over hook again and pull it through the two remaining loops.

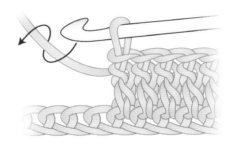

4 You will be left with one loop on the hook. Continue working one double crochet in each chain to the end of the foundation chain.

5 Then turn the work to begin the next row. Make three chain. Work one double crochet in each double crochet in the row below to the end of the row.

6 For all subsequent rows, repeat Step 5.

Loop stitch

1 With the yarn over the left index finger, insert the hook into the next stitch and draw two strands through the stitch (take the first strand from under the index finger and at the same time take the second strand from over the index finger).

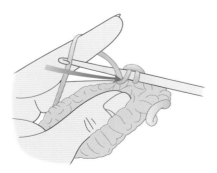

2 Pull the yarn to tighten the loop, forming a 1-in (2.5-cm) loop on the index finger. Remove your finger from the loop, keeping the loop to the back (wrong side) of the work, yarn over hook and pull through three loops on the hook (one loop stitch made on wrong side of work).

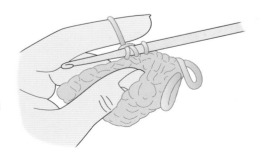

Increasing

You can increase by working two or three stitches into one stitch or space from the previous row. The illustration shows a two-stitch increase being made in double crochet.

Half double 2 stitches together (hdc2tog)

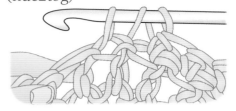

1 Yarn over hook, insert hook into next stitch, yarn over hook, draw yarn through (three loops on the hook).

Decreasing

You can decrease by missing the next stitch and continuing to crochet, or by crocheting two or more stitches together. The basic technique for crocheting stitches together is the same for all stitches.

Single crochet 2 stitches together (sc2tog)

1 Insert the hook into the work, yarn over hook and pull through the work (two loops on hook), insert the hook in the next stitch, yarn over hook and pull the yarn through.

2 Yarn over hook again and pull through all three loops on the hook. You will then have one loop on the hook.

2 Yarn over hook, insert hook into next stitch, yarn over hook, draw yarn through.

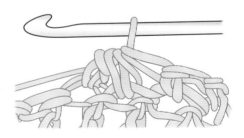

3 Draw yarn through all five loops on the hook.

Five-double crochet cluster (5dcCL)

The five-double crochet cluster creates a bobble on the right side of the work. You begin by working on the wrong side, and the bobble is pushed out toward the right side.

*yarn over hook, insert hook into next stitch, yarn over hook, pull yarn through, yarn over hook, pull through two loops, repeat from * four times more, yarn over hook, pull yarn through all six loops on hook.

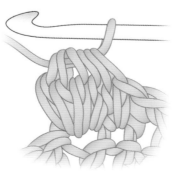

Sewing seams

Join the seams together by picking up the loops at the top of the stitches of corresponding pieces and working an overcast stitch.

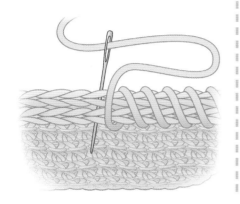

Single crochet seam

With a single crochet seam you join two pieces together using a crochet hook and working a single crochet stitch through both pieces, instead of sewing them together with a tail of yarn and a yarn sewing needle. This makes a quick and strong seam and gives a slightly raised finish to the edging.

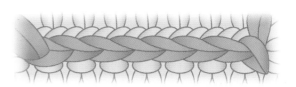

1 Start by lining up the two pieces with wrong sides together. Insert the hook in the top two loops of the stitch of the first piece, then into the corresponding stitch on the second piece.

2 Complete the single crochet stitch as normal and continue on next stitches as directed in the pattern. This gives a raised effect if the single crochet stitches are made on the right side of the work.

Making pompoms   Book method

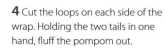

1 Leaving a long tail, wrap the yarn around a paperback book (or something a similar size) about 120 times, leaving a second long tail.

2 Ease the wrapped yarn off the book gently and wrap the second tail tightly around the center six or seven times.

3 Take a yarn sewing needle and thread in the second tail. Push the needle through the center wrap backward and forward three or four times.

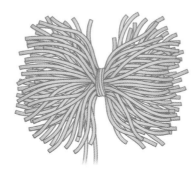

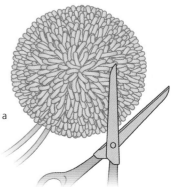

4 Cut the loops on each side of the wrap. Holding the two tails in one hand, fluff the pompom out.

5 Hold the pompom in one hand and use sharp scissors to trim it into a round and even shape.

Adding safety eyes

Safety eyes are a great choice to add character to your hat, but only when there is a padded or stuffed area behind the eye, as the backs of the eyes can be a little uncomfortable against the head without a barrier. If you prefer you can embroider eyes after the hat is completed.

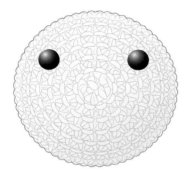

Insert the safety eyes in place on the face from the right side.

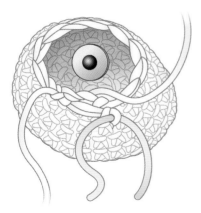

Make sure they are completely level and sitting on the same row before you secure the safety catches at the back. The flat piece of the safety catch is pushed toward the crochet piece from the inside.

Embroidery stitches

Here are some useful stitches for adding features to your animal hats. I used straight stitches for whiskers and mouths and for appliquéing on eyes (see the baby panda on page 46), satin stitch for noses and French knots for pupils.

Straight stitch

These are single straight stitches that are not placed in a straight line but used at an appropriate angle to create eyelashes, a nose, or a mouth.

Satin stitch

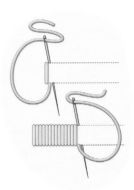

To work satin stitch, it can help to outline the shape you want to fill first. Then begin at one end of the shape and work straight stitches from side to side, placed very close together and varying their length as required to create a solid shape.

Tips

When sewing on small pieces such as the nose, use a yarn sewing needle with a sharp end.

When making ears and nose details for the faces, leave ends long for sewing onto hat when fastening off.

French knots

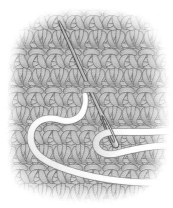

1 Thread the yarn into a yarn sewing needle. Bring the yarn out at your starting point from the back of the work to the front and where you want the French knot to sit, leaving a tail of yarn at the back that you will sew in later. Pick up a couple of strands across the stitch on the front of the work close to the place the yarn has been pulled through.

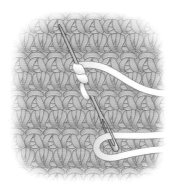

2 Wrap the yarn round the needle two or three times, pushing the wraps close to the crochet piece.

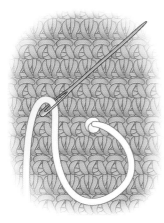

3 Take the needle in one hand and pull it through the wraps, holding the wraps in place near the crochet piece with the other hand. This will form a little knot close to the crochet piece.

4 Insert the needle (from the right side) very close to the knot and push the needle through to the wrong side (French knot made).

Crochet stitch conversion chart

Crochet stitches are worked in the same way in both the USA and the UK, but the stitch names are not the same and identical names are used for different stitches. Below is a list of the US terms used in this book, and the equivalent UK terms.

US TERM	UK TERM
single crochet (sc)	double crochet (dc)
half double crochet (hdc)	half treble (htr)
double crochet (dc)	treble (tr)
treble (tr)	double treble (dtr)
double treble (dtr)	triple treble (trtr)
triple treble (trtr)	quadruple treble (qtr)
gauge	tension
yarn over hook (yoh)	yarn round hook (yrh)

chapter 1
cute baby hats

Herbie the rabbit

This baby rabbit has lovely floppy ears—and with its cute little button nose, it's very hard to resist!

Materials

Debbie Bliss Cashmerino Aran, 55% merino wool, 33% acrylic, 12% cashmere worsted (aran) yarn, 1¾oz (50g) balls, approx 98yd (90m) per ball:
   2 x balls of shade 027 Stone (light gray) (MC)

Debbie Bliss Rialto DK, 100% merino wool light worsted (DK) yarn, 1¾oz (50g) balls, approx 115yd (105m) per ball:
   1 x ball of shade 42 Pink (A)

Debbie Bliss Rialto Chunky, 100% merino wool bulky (chunky) yarn, 1¾oz (50g) balls, approx 66yd (60m) per ball:
   Scrap of shade 001 Black (B)

US size 7 (4.5mm) and US size E/4 (3.5mm) crochet hooks

Yarn sewing needle

Gauge

15 sts x 11 rows over a 4in (10cm) square using US size 7 (4.5mm) hook, half double crochet, and Cashmerino Aran.

Size

To fit age 6–24 months

Finished measurements

Approx 16–18in (40.5–46cm) circumference, 6½in (16.5cm) high

Abbreviations

approx approximately
beg begin(ning)
ch chain
hdc half double crochet
rep repeat
RS right side
sc single crochet
ss slip stitch
st(s) stitch(es)
WS wrong side

Hat

Work in rounds, placing st marker at beg of each round.
Round 1: Using MC and US size 7 (4.5mm) hook, 2ch, 8hdc in second ch from hook. (*8 sts*)
Round 2: 2hdc in each st to end. (*16 sts*)
Round 3: *2hdc in next st, 1hdc in next st; rep from * to end. (*24 sts*)
Round 4: *2hdc in next st, 1hdc in each of next 2 sts; rep from * to end. (*32 sts*)
Round 5: *2hdc in next st, 1hdc in each of next 3 sts; rep from * to end. (*40 sts*)
Round 6: *2hdc in next st, 1hdc in each of next 4 sts; rep from * to end. (*48 sts*)
Round 7: *2hdc in next st, 1hdc in each of next 5 sts; rep from * to end. (*56 sts*)
Round 8: *2hdc in next st, 1hdc in each of next 6 sts; rep from * to end. (*64 sts*)
Rounds 9–19: 1hdc in each st to end. (*64 sts*)
Ss in next st.
Fasten off.

Outer ear

(*make 2*)
Work in rows, turning at end of each row.
Row 1: Using MC and US size 7 (4.5mm) hook, make 2ch, 3sc in second ch from hook. Turn. (*3 sts*)
Row 2: 1ch (does not count as a st throughout), 2sc in first st, 1sc in next st, 2sc in last st. (*5 sts*)
Row 3: 1ch, 1sc in each st to end. (*5 sts*)
Row 4: 1ch, 2sc in first st, 1sc in each of next 3 sts, 2sc in last st. (*7 sts*)
Row 5: 1ch, 1sc in each st to end. (*7 sts*)
Row 6: 1ch, 2sc in first st, 1sc in each of next 5 sts, 2sc in last st. (*9 sts*)
Row 7: 1ch, 1sc in each st to end. (*9 sts*)
Row 8: 1ch, 2sc in first st, 1sc in each of next 7 sts, 2sc in last st. (*11 sts*)
Row 9: 1ch, 1sc in each st to end. (*11 sts*)
Row 10: 1ch, 2sc in first st, 1sc in each of next 9 sts, 2sc in last st. (*13 sts*)
Rows 11–25: 1ch, 1sc in each st to end. (*13 sts*)
Fasten off, leaving a long tail for sewing Inner ear to Outer ear.

Inner ear
(make 2)

Work in rows, turning at end of each row.

Row 1: Using A and US size E/4 (3.5mm) hook, make 2ch, 3sc in second ch from hook. Turn. (3 sts)

Row 2: 1ch (does not count as st throughout), 2sc in first st, 1sc in next st, 2sc in last st. (5 sts)

Rows 3–4: 1ch, 1sc in each st to end. (5 sts)

Row 5: 1ch, 2sc in first st, 1sc in each of next 3 sts, 2sc in last st. (7 sts)

Rows 6–7: 1ch, 1sc in each st to end. (7 sts)

Row 8: 1ch, 2sc in first st, 1sc in each of next 5 sts, 2sc in last st. (9 sts)

Rows 9–25: 1ch, 1sc in each st to end. (9 sts)

Fasten off.

With RS together, pin and sew outside edges of Inner ear and Outer ear together leaving bottom edge open. Turn RS out. Position ears on top of Hat, approx 1in (2.5cm) apart at top. Shape outer edges of ears towards middle, and pin and sew in place.

Eyes

Using B, embroider eyes in satin stitch (see page 18), approx 5 sts from each side of center of hat and approx 9 rows up from bottom edge.

Nose

Work in rows, turning at end of each row.

Row 1: Using A and US size E/4 (3.5mm) hook, make 2ch, 3sc in second ch from hook. Turn. (3 sts)

Row 2: 1ch (does not count as st throughout), 1sc in each st. (3 sts)

Row 3: 1ch, 2sc in first st, 1sc in next st, 2sc in last st. (5 sts)

Fasten off, leaving long yarn tail for sewing to hat.

Sew Nose to Hat between eyes, with tip of triangle facing downwards and approx 5 rows from bottom edging.

Mouth

Using B, embroider the mouth in straight stitch (see page 18), using the photo as a guide.

Tips

When sewing on small pieces such as the Nose, use a yarn sewing needle with a sharp end.

When making ears and nose details for the faces, leave ends long for sewing onto hat when fastening off.

I just think this is the cutest little hat—and it makes a great present for a baby or toddler.

Evie the duck

Debbie Bliss Rialto DK, 100% merino wool light worsted (DK) yarn, 1¾oz (50g) balls, approx 115yd (105m) per ball:
    Small amount of shade 34 Fuchsia (dark pink) (C)
    Scrap of shade 03 Black

US size H/8 (5mm) and US size E/4 (3.5mm) crochet hooks

Yarn sewing needle

Gauge
15 sts x 11 rows over a 4in (10cm) square using US size H/8 (5mm) hook, half double crochet, and Cashmerino Aran.

Size
To fit age 6–24 months

Finished measurements
Approx 16–18in (40.5–46cm) circumference, 6½in (16.5cm) high

Abbreviations
approx approximately
beg begin(ning)
ch chain
dc double crochet
hdc half double crochet
rep repeat
RS right side
sc single crochet
ss slip stitch
st(s) stitch(es)
tr treble
WS wrong side

Materials
Debbie Bliss Cashmerino Aran, 55% merino wool, 33% acrylic, 12% cashmere worsted (aran) yarn, 1¾oz (50g) balls, approx 98yd (90m) per ball:
    1 x ball of shade 064 Cowslip (yellow) (MC)

Debbie Bliss Baby Cashmerino, 55% wool, 33% acrylic, 12% cashmere sportweight (4ply) yarn, 1¾oz (50g) balls, approx 137yd (125m) per ball:
    Small amounts each of shade 092 Orange (A), shade 101 Ecru (off white) (B)

Hat
Work in rounds, placing st marker at beg of each round.
Round 1: Using MC and US size H/8 (5mm) hook, 2ch, 8hdc in second ch from hook. (8 sts)
Round 2: 2hdc in each st. (16 sts)
Round 3: *1hdc in next st, 2hdc in next st; rep from * to end. (24 sts)
Round 4: *1hdc in each of next 2 sts, 2hdc in next st; rep from * to end. (32 sts)
Round 5: *1hdc in each of next 3 sts, 2hdc in next st; rep from * to end. (40 sts)
Round 6: *1hdc in each of next 4 sts, 2hdc in next st; rep from * to end. (48 sts)
Round 7: *1hdc in each of next 5 sts, 2hdc in next st; rep from * to end. (56 sts)
Round 8: *1hdc in each of next 6 sts, 2hdc in next st; rep from * to end. (64 sts)
Rounds 9–19: 1hdc in each st to end. (64 sts) or until work measures approx 6½in (16.5cm) from start.
Next round: 1sc in each st, ss in last st.
Fasten off.

Beak
Work in rounds, placing st marker at beg of each round.
Round 1 (RS): Using A and US size E/4 (3.5mm) hook, make 2ch, 4sc in second ch from hook. (4 sts)
Round 2: 2sc in each st to end. (8 sts)
Round 3: 2sc in each st to end. (16 sts)
Round 4: 2sc in each st to end. (32 sts)
Rounds 5–6: 1sc in each st to end.
Round 7: Ss in each st to end.
Fasten off, leaving long end for sewing up.

Sew in end in center of beak on WS.
Fold in half with WS together and with fasten off st on one side.
Sew beak together slightly at each edge approx 2 sts on each side.
Center Beak at bottom edge and sew straight edge of beak onto right side of Hat (leaving beak open).

Eyes
Using scrap of black yarn, embroider eyes in satin stitch (see page 18) approx 6 rows up from bottom edge and approx 5 sts apart.

Head feathers

Make 5 "feather" strands using chains and ss around Round 2 at top of Hat as follows:

Using MC and US size E/4 (3.5mm) hook, join yarn at top of hat in any st of Round 2 of Hat by picking up 2 loops of st, *make 8ch, ss in second ch from hook and each of following 7 ch, ss in another two loops of one of sts in same round; rep from * 3 times more, ending with a ss in same place as beginning joining st.

Fasten off.

Sew in ends.

Flower

Work in rounds, placing st marker at beg of each round.

Using B and US size E/4 (3.5mm) hook, make 4ch, join with a ss in first ch to form a ring.

Round 1 (RS): 1ch, 6sc in ring, break off B.

Round 2: Join C with a ss in first sc, *[4ch, 1tr, 4ch, 1ss] in same st, ss in next st; rep from * 5 times more (6 petals), working last ss in sc at base of first 4ch.

Fasten off.

Sew Flower onto Face, using the photo as a guide.

Nugget the mouse

Little round ears and a cute nose! The nose is stuffed with polyester filling, or use yarn ends.

Materials

Debbie Bliss Cashmerino Aran, 55% merino wool, 33% acrylic, 12% cashmere worsted (aran) yarn, 1¾oz (50g) balls, approx 98yd (90m) per ball:
    1 x ball of shade 09 Grey (MC)
    Small amount of shade 079 Nude (pale pink) (A)

Louisa Harding Cassia, 75% wool, 25% nylon light worsted (DK) yarn, 1¾oz (50g) balls, approx 145yd (133m) per ball:
    Scrap of shade 124 Coral (B)

Debbie Bliss Rialto DK, 100% merino wool light worsted (DK) yarn, 1¾oz (50g) balls, approx 115yd (105m) per ball:
    Scrap of shade 01 White (C)
    Scrap of shade 03 Black (D)

US size H/8 (5mm) and US size E/4 (3.5mm) crochet hooks

Yarn sewing needle

Polyester toy stuffing

Gauge

15 sts x 11 rows over a 4in (10cm) square using US size H/8 (5mm) hook, single crochet, and Cashmerino Aran.

Size

To fit age 6–24 months

Finished measurements

Approx 16–18in (40.5–46cm) circumference, 6½in (16.5cm) high

Abbreviations

approx approximately
beg begin(ning)
ch chain
cont continue
dc double crochet
foll following
hdc half double crochet
rep repeat
RS right side
sc single crochet
ss slip stitch
st(s) stitch(es)
WS wrong side

Hat

Work in rounds, placing st marker at beg of each round.
Round 1: Using MC and US size H/8 (5mm) hook, 2ch, 8hdc in second ch from hook. (*8 sts*)
Round 2: 2hdc in each st. (*16 sts*)
Round 3: *1hdc in next st, 2hdc in next st; rep from * to end. (*24 sts*)
Round 4: *1hdc in each of next 2 sts, 2hdc in next st; rep from * to end. (*32 sts*)
Round 5: *1hdc in each of next 3 sts, 2hdc in next st; rep from * to end. (*40 sts*)
Round 6: *1hdc in each of next 4 sts, 2hdc in next st; rep from * to end. (*48 sts*)
Round 7: *1hdc in each of next 5 sts, 2hdc in next st; rep from * to end. (*56 sts*)
Round 8: *1hdc in each of next 6 sts, 2hdc in next st; rep from * to end. (*64 sts*)
Rounds 9–19: 1hdc in each st to end. (*64 sts*) or until work measures approx 6½in (16.5cm) from start.
Next round: 1sc in each st, ss in last st.
Fasten off.

Ears

(*make 4*)
Work in rounds, placing st marker at beg of each round.
Using A and US size H/8 (5mm) hook, make 4ch, join with a ss to form a ring.

Round 1: 1ch, 12sc in ring, cut A, using MC, join with a ss in first sc. (*12 sts*)
Round 2: Cont with MC, 1ch, 2sc in same st as ss and each foll st to end, join with a ss in first sc. (*24 sts*)
Round 3: 1ch, 1sc in same st as ss, 1sc in each of next 2 sts, 2sc in next st, *1sc in each of next 3 sts, 2sc in next st; rep from * to end, join with a ss in first sc. (*30 sts*)
Round 4: 1ch, 1sc in first st, 1sc in each following st to end. Join with a ss in first sc. (*30 sts*)
Fasten off leaving a long tail for sewing on later.
Sew around hole in center and pull to close.

Place two Ears with WS together, then sew Ears on at center top of Hat approx 3in (7.5cm) apart and starting approx 4 rounds down from top.

Eyes

Using D, embroider eyes in satin stitch (see page 18), using D, approx 1 row above nose and 7 sts apart.

Nose

Work in rounds, placing st marker at beg of each round.
Round 1: Using MC and US size E/4 (3.5mm) hook, 2ch, 4sc in second ch from hook. (*4 sts*)
Round 2: 2sc in each st to end. (*8 sts*)
Round 3: *1sc in next st, 2sc in next st; rep from * to end. (*12 sts*)
Round 4: *1sc in each of next 2 sts, 2sc in next st; rep from * to end. (*16 sts*)

Round 5: *1sc in each of next 3 sts, 2sc in next st; rep from * to end. *(20 sts)*

Rounds 6–8: 1sc in each st to end.

Fasten off, leaving a long tail for sewing on.

Nose tip

Using B and US size E/4 (3.5mm) hook, make 2ch, 5dc in second ch from hook.

Fasten off, leaving a long end.

Sew around opening to close and make into a bobble shape. Sew onto tip of Nose.

Stuff nose, position in center of Hat at bottom edge and sew in place. Using C, sew 3 whiskers in straight stitch (see page 18) on each side of nose, using the photo as a guide.

Hannah the kitten

Lovely long whiskers and a cute pink bow make this an adorable little kitten hat.

Materials

Debbie Bliss Cashmerino Aran, 55% merino wool, 33% acrylic, 12% cashmere worsted (aran) yarn, 1¾oz (50g) balls, approx 98yd (90m) per ball:
  1 x ball of shade 101 Ecru (off white) (MC)

Debbie Bliss Rialto DK, 100% merino wool light worsted (DK) yarn, 1¾oz (50g) balls, approx 115yd (105m) per ball:
  1 x ball of shade 42 Pink (A)
  Scrap of shade 01 Black (B)

Louisa Harding Cassia, 75% wool, 25% nylon light worsted (DK) yarn, 1¾oz (50g) balls, approx 145yd (133m) per ball:
  Scrap of shade 124 Coral (C)

US size H/8 (5mm) and US size E/4 (3.5mm) crochet hooks

Yarn sewing needle

Gauge

15 sts x 11 rows over a 4in (10cm) square using US size H/8 (5mm) hook, half double crochet, and Cashmerino Aran.

Size

To fit age 6–24 months

Finished measurements

Approx 16–18in (40.5–46cm) circumference, 6½in (16.5cm) high

Abbreviations

approx approximately
beg beginning
ch chain
dc double crochet
hdc half double crochet
rep repeat
RS right side
sc single crochet
ss slip stitch
st(s) stitch(es)
WS wrong side

Hat

Work in rounds, placing st marker at beg of each round.
Round 1: Using MC and US size H/8 (5mm) hook, 2ch, 8hdc in second ch from hook. (8 sts)
Round 2: 2hdc in each st. (16 sts)
Round 3: *1hdc in next st, 2hdc in next st; rep from * to end. (24 sts)
Round 4: *1hdc in each of next 2 sts, 2hdc in next st; rep from * to end. (32 sts)
Round 5: *1hdc in each of next 3 sts, 2hdc in next st; rep from * to end. (40 sts)
Round 6: *1hdc in each of next 4 sts, 2hdc in next st; rep from * to end. (48 sts)
Round 7: *1hdc in each of next 5 sts, 2hdc in next st; rep from * to end. (56 sts)
Round 8: *1hdc in each of next 6 sts, 2hdc in next st; rep from * to end. (64 sts)
Rounds 9–19: 1hdc in each st to end. (64 sts) or until work measures approx 6½in (16.5cm) from start.
Next round: 1sc in each st, ss in last st.
Fasten off.

Ears

(make 2)
Work in rounds, placing st marker at beg of each round.
Round 1: Using MC and US size H/8 (5mm) hook, 2ch, 4sc in second ch from hook. (4 sts)
Round 2: 2sc in each st to end. (8 sts)
Round 3: *1sc in each of next 3 sts, 2sc in next st; rep from * to end. (10 sts)
Round 4: *1sc in each of next 4 sts, 2sc in next st; rep from * to end. (12 sts)
Round 5: *1sc n each of next 5 sts, 2sc in next st; rep from * to end. (14 sts)
Round 6: *1sc in each of next 6 sts, 2sc in next st; rep from * to end. (16 sts)
Round 7: *1sc in each of next 7 sts, 2sc in next st; rep from * to end. (18 sts)
Round 8: *1sc in each of next 8 sts, 2sc in next st; rep from * to end. (20 sts)
Ss in next st.
Fasten off, leaving long tail for sewing on.

With straight edges of Ears flat, start sewing them at center top of Hat approx 3in (7.5cm) apart and starting 4 rounds down from top.

Eyes

Using B, embroider eyes in satin stitch (see page 18) approx 6 rows up from bottom edge and approx 11 sts apart.

Nose

Work in rows, turning at end of each row.

Row 1: Using A and US size E/4 (3.5mm) hook, make 2ch, 3sc in second ch from hook. Turn. (*3 sts*)

Row 2: 1ch, 1sc in each st. (*3 sts*)

Fasten off, leaving a long tail for sewing on.

Sew in ends carefully, neatening up triangle shape.

Center Nose onto Hat, with bottom point positioned approx 2 rows up from bottom of hat.

Using B, embroider 3 whiskers in straight stitch (see page 18) on each side of hat, using the photo as a guide.

Bow

Work in rounds, placing st marker at beg of each round.

Using C and US size E/4 (3.5mm) hook, make 16ch and join with a ss in first ch to form a ring.

Round 1 (RS): 1ch (does not count as a st), 1sc in each ch to end, join with a ss in first sc. (*16 sts*)

Round 2: 3ch (counts as first dc), 1dc in each st to end; join with a ss in top of first 3–ch. (*16 sts*)

Round 3: 1ch, 1sc in each st to end, join with a ss in first sc.

Fasten off, leaving a yarn tail approx 17½in (45cm) long.

With RS facing, hold piece flat with fasten-off stitch and tail at center top at front. Wrap yarn tail tightly around center of ring 5 or 6 times to create bow shape, and secure in place with yarn tail and yarn sewing needle.

Attach Bow at top of Hat between center and one Ear, using the photo as a guide.

Cheeky and extremely cute.
A great hat for wearing whilst
practicing tiger roars.

Neal
the tiger

Materials

Debbie Bliss Rialto DK, 100% merino wool light
worsted (DK) yarn, 1¾oz (50g) balls, approx 115yd
(105m) per ball:

  1 x ball of shade 03 Black (A)
  1 x ball of shade 43 Burnt Orange (B)
  1 x ball of shade 02 Ecru (C)

US size E/4 (3.5mm) crochet hook

Yarn sewing needle

Gauge

16 sts x 13 rows over a 4in (10cm) square using US
size E/4 (3.5mm) hook, half double crochet, and
Rialto DK.

Size

To fit age 6–24 months

Finished measurements

Approx 16–18in 40.5–46cm) circumference,
6½in (16.5cm) high

Abbreviations

approx approximately
beg beginning
ch chain
cont continue
hdc half double crochet
rep repeat
RS right side
sc single crochet
ss slip stitch
st(s) stitch(es)

Tips

This hat is worked from the bottom
to the top. It has a mix of rounds and
rows, so check carefully when rounds turn
into rows and rows turn into rounds, and
use stitch markers to mark the beginning
of each round.

The stripe is made up of 2 rows of
orange and 1 row black.

Hat

Lower section:

Work in rounds.

Foundation chain: Using B, make 73ch, join with ss in first ch. Insert st marker.

Round 1 (RS): 1ch (does not count as st), 1sc in next and each following ch to end. *(72 sts)*

Cut yarn and change to B in top of last st, so you are ready to start next round using B. Insert st marker.

NOTE: When changing color, cut yarn and change yarn in top of last st, so you are ready to start next round using new color. Insert st marker.

Keep color changes on top of each other as you go up rounds, so that joins remain in line from top to bottom of Hat and at back. Now work in spirals.

Round 2: Using B, 1hdc in each st to end. *(72 sts)*

Round 3: Using B, 1hdc in each st to end. *(72 sts)*

Round 4: Using A, 1hdc in each st to end. *(72 sts)*

Cont to use color sequence from Rounds 2–4 (two rounds B, one round A) throughout pattern.

Rounds 5–10: 1hdc in each st to end. *(72 sts)*

Middle section:

Round 11: 1hdc in each of next 23 sts. Insert st marker. 1hdc in each of next 23 sts. Insert st marker. These two st markers mark beg and end of open part of Face. 1hdc in each of next 49 sts. Turn.

Working on these 49 sts only in rows (not rounds), changing color at back of work and using color sequence of two rows B, one row A as before:

Row 12: 2ch (does not count as st), 1hdc in each of next 49 sts. Turn. *(49 sts)*

Row 13: 2ch (does not count as st), 1hdc in each of next 49 sts. Do not turn.

Cont in rounds.

Round 14: Make 23ch, skip next 23 sts (from Round 8), skip first 2-ch (from start of Row 10), 1hdc in each of next 25 sts (ending at center back of hat).

Insert st marker to mark start of next round.

Round 15: 1hdc in each of next 24 sts, 1hdc in each of next 23 ch, 1hdc in each of next 25 sts. *(72 sts—it's very important to have correct number of sts at end of this round)*

Round 16: Use A on this round. Do not change color when you get to B sts used on front 23 ch, cont using A. 1hdc in each st to end. *(72 sts)*

Round 17: 1hdc in each st to end. *(72 sts)*

Top section:

Beg decreases.

Cont following rounds, changing color at join in line from bottom to top of Hat.

Round 18: *1hdc in each of next 10 sts, hdc2tog; rep from * to end. *(66 sts)*

Round 19: *1hdc in each of next 9 sts, hdc2tog; rep from * to end. *(60 sts)*

Round 20: *1hdc in each of next 8 sts, hdc2tog; rep from * to end. *(54 sts)*

Round 21: *1hdc in each of next 7 sts, hdc2tog; rep from * to end. *(48 sts)*

Round 22: *1hdc in each of next 6 sts, hdc2tog; rep from * to end. *(42 sts)*

Round 23: *1hdc in each of next 5 sts, hdc2tog; rep from * to end. *(36 sts)*

Round 24: *1hdc in each of next 4 sts, hdc2tog; rep from * to end. *(30 sts)*

Round 25: *1hdc in each of next 3 sts, hdc2tog; rep from * to end. *(24 sts)*

Round 26: *1hdc in each of next 2 sts, hdc2tog; rep from * to end. *(18 sts)*

Round 27: *1hdc in next st, hdc2tog; rep from * to end. *(12 sts)*

Round 28: Hdc2tog around. *(6 sts)*

Fasten off.

Face edging:

With RS facing, join C in first st of bottom face edge.

1ch, 1sc in same st, 1sc in each of next 22 sts, 7sc evenly along side of face edge, 21sc evenly along top of face edge, 7sc evenly along other side of face edge, join with a ss in first sc.

Ears

(make 2)

Work in rounds, placing st marker at beg of each round.

Round 1: Using C, make 2ch, 6sc in second ch from hook.

Round 2: 2sc in each st to end. *(12 sts)*

Round 3: *1sc in each of next 2 sts, 2sc in next st; rep from * to end. *(16 sts)*

Cut yarn, join B.

Round 4: Cont with B, *1sc in each of next 3 sts, 2sc in next st; rep from * to end. *(20 sts)*

Rounds 5–8: 1sc in each st to end. *(20 sts)*

Ss in next st.

Fasten off, leaving a long tail for sewing on.

Pin each Ear onto hat starting approx 3 rows down from top center of Hat and sew in place.

Fernando the lion

This is an adorable lion. The mane not only looks fun, it makes for extra insulation too.

Materials

Debbie Bliss Falkland Aran, 100% wool aran (worsted) yarn, 100g (3½oz) hanks, approx 197yd (180m) per hank:

   1 x hank of shade 07 Mustard (yellow) (MC)

Debbie Bliss Cashmerino Aran, 55% merino wool, 33% acrylic, 12% cashmere worsted (aran) yarn, 1¾oz (50g) balls, approx 98yd (90m) per ball:

   1 x ball of shade 066 Mustard (A)

US size G/6 (4mm) crochet hook

Gauge

15 sts x 11 rows over a 4in (10cm) square using US size G/6 (4mm) hook, half double crochet, and Falkland Aran.

Size

To fit age 6–24 months

Finished measurements

Approx 16–18in (40.5–46cm) circumference, 6½in (16.5cm) high

Abbreviations

approx approximately
beg begin(ning)
ch chain
cont continue
dc double crochet
hdc half double crochet
rep repeat
RS right side
sc single crochet
ss slip stitch
st(s) stitch(es)

Hat

Lower section:
Work in rounds.
Foundation chain: Using MC, make 73ch, join with a ss in first ch. Insert st marker.
Round 1 (RS): 1ch (does not count as a st), 1sc in next and each following ch to end. (72 *sts*)
Insert st marker.
Work in spirals.
Rounds 2–7: 1hdc in each st to end. (72 *sts*)

Middle section:
Round 8: 1hdc in each of next 23 sts. Insert st marker. 1hdc in each of next 23 sts. Insert st marker. These two st markers mark beg and end of open part of Face. 1hdc in each of next 49 sts. Turn. Working on these 49 sts only, work in rows (not rounds).
Row 9: 2ch (does not count as st), 1hdc in each of next 49 sts, turn. (49 *sts*)
Row 10: 2ch (does not count as st), 1hdc in each of next 49 sts. Do not turn. (49 *sts*)
Cont in rounds.
Round 11: Make 23ch, skip next 23 sts (from Round 8), skip first 2ch (from start of Row 10), 1hdc in next 25 sts (ending at center back of hat).
Insert st marker to mark start of next round.
Round 12: 1hdc in each of next 24 sts, 1hdc in each of next 23 ch, 1hdc in each of next 25 sts. (72 *sts*—it's very important to have correct number of sts at end of this round)
Rounds 13–14: 1hdc in each st to end. (72 *sts*)

Top section:

Beg decreases.

Round 15: *1hdc in each of next 10 sts, hdc2tog; rep from * to end. *(66 sts)*

Round 16: *1hdc in each of next 9 sts, hdc2tog; rep from * to end. *(60 sts)*

Round 17: *1hdc in each of next 8 sts, hdc2tog; rep from * to end. *(54 sts)*

Round 18: *1hdc in each of next 7 sts, hdc2tog; rep from * to end. *(48 sts)*

Round 19: *1hdc in each of next 6 sts, hdc2tog; rep from * to end. *(42 sts)*

Round 20: *1hdc in each of next 5 sts, hdc2tog; rep from * to end. *(36 sts)*

Round 21: *1hdc in each of next 4 sts, hdc2tog; rep from * to end. *(30 sts)*

Round 22: *1hdc in each of next 3 sts, hdc2tog; rep from * to end. *(24 sts)*

Round 23: *1hdc in each of next 2 sts, hdc2tog; rep from * to end. *(18 sts)*

Round 24: *1hdc in next st, hdc2tog; rep from * to end. *(12 sts)*

Round 25: Hdc2tog around. *(6 sts)*

Fasten off.

Face edging:

With RS facing, join MC in first st of bottom face edge.

1ch, 1sc in same st, 1sc in each of next 22 sts, 7sc evenly along side of face edge, 21sc evenly along top of face edge, 7sc evenly along other side of face edge, join with a ss in first sc.

Ears

(make 2)

Work in rounds, placing st marker at beg of each round.

Round 1: Using MC, make 2ch, 6sc in second ch from hook.

Round 2: 2sc in each st to end. *(12 sts)*

Round 3: *1sc in each of next 2 sts, 2sc in next st; rep from * to end. *(16 sts)*

Round 4: *1sc in each of next 3 sts, 2sc in next st; rep from * to end. *(20 sts)*

Rounds 5–8: 1sc in each st to end. *(20 sts)*

Ss in next st.

Fasten off, leaving long tail for sewing on.

Pin each Ear onto hat approx 3 rows down from top center of Hat and sew in place.

Mane

Using A, cut approx 200 strands of yarn each approx 5in (12.5cm) long and make one-strand tassels in shape of Lion's mane from top of Hat, approx 2 rows around front of Ears and 2 rows around back, around sides, along bottom (3 rows from opening).

Note

This hat is worked from the bottom to the top. It has a mix of rounds and rows, so check carefully when rounds turn into rows and rows turn into rounds, and use stitch markers to mark the beginning of each round.

A very sweet and cheeky raccoon, which would make an ideal gift.

Roger the raccoon

Materials

Debbie Bliss Cashmerino Aran, 55% merino wool, 33% acrylic, 12% cashmere worsted (aran) yarn, 1¾oz (50g) balls, approx 98yd (90m) per ball:

    1 x ball of shade 09 Grey (MC)
    1 x ball of shade 101 Ecru (off white) (A)
    1 x ball of shade 300 Black (B)

US size H/8 (5mm) and US size E/4 (3.5mm) crochet hooks

Yarn sewing needle

Gauge

15 sts x 11 rows over a 4in (10cm) square using US size H/8 (5mm) hook, half double crochet, and Cashmerino Aran.

Size

To fit age 6–24 months

Finished measurements

Approx 16–18in (40.5–46cm) circumference, 6½in (16.5cm) high

Abbreviations

approx approximately
ch chain
cont continue
hdc half double crochet
rep repeat
RS right side
sc single crochet
sc2tog single crochet 2 stitches together
ss slip stitch
st(s) stitch(es)
WS wrong side

Hat

Work in rounds, placing st marker at beg of each round.

Round 1: Using MC and US size H/8 (5mm) hook, 2ch, 6hdc in second ch from hook. (6 sts)

Rounds 2–3: 2hdc in each st. (24 sts)

Round 4: *1hdc in each of next 2 sts, 2hdc in next st; rep from * to end. (32 sts)

Round 5: *1hdc in each of next 3 sts, 2hdc in next st; rep from * to end. (40 sts)

Round 6: *1hdc in each of next 4 sts, 2hdc in next st; rep from * to end. (48 sts)

Round 7: *1hdc in each of next 5 sts, 2hdc in next st; rep from * to end. (56 sts)

Rounds 8–19: 1hdc in each st to end. (56 sts) or until work measures approx 6½in (16.5cm) from start. Do not fasten off. Place first st marker here to denote center back of Hat.

First earflap:

Using MC, 1sc in each of next 6 sts. Cut MC. Do not turn. Beg working in rows, turning at end of each following row.

Row 1 (RS): Join A, 1sc in each of next 13 sts. Turn. (13 sts)

Row 2 (WS): 1ch (does not count as st throughout), sc2tog, 1sc in each of next 9 sts, sc2tog. (11 sts)
Cut A, join B.

Row 3: 1sc in each st to end. (11 sts)

Row 4: 1ch, sc2tog, 1sc in each of next 7 sts, sc2tog. (9 sts)
Cut B, join A.

Row 5: 1sc in each st to end. (9 sts)

Row 6: 1ch, sc2tog, 1sc in each of next 5 sts, sc2tog. (7 sts)
Cut A, join B.

Row 7: 1ch, 1sc in each st to end. (7 sts)

Row 8: 1ch, 1sc in each st to end. (7 sts)
Cut B, join A.

Row 9: 1sc in each st to end. (7 sts)

Row 10: 1ch, sc2tog, 1sc in each of next 3 sts, sc2tog. (*5 sts*)
Cut A, join B.
Row 11: 1sc in each st to end. (*5 sts*)
Row 12: 1ch, sc2tog, 1sc in next st, sc2tog. (*3 sts*)
Do not cut yarn, cont with B.
Row 13: 1ch, 1sc in each st to end. (*3 sts*)
Fasten off.

Second earflap:
With RS facing, join MC in next st along from end of Row 1 of First earflap.
1ch, 1sc in same st, 1sc in each of next 8 sts, place second st marker here to denote center front of hat, 1sc in each of next 10 sts. Do not turn. Cut MC. (*19 sts*)
Work in rows, turning at end of each following row.
Row 1 (RS): Join A, 1sc in each of next 13 sts. Turn.
Rep Rows 2–13 of First earflap.

Using MC, with RS facing, join yarn in Hat edge in same st as last st at end of Row 1 of Second earflap, 1ch, 1sc in each of next 11 sts, ss in next st.
Fasten off.
Sew in ends.

Face
(*make two*)
Work in rows, turning at end of each row.
Row 1: Using A and 5mm (US size H/8) hook, make 2ch, 2sc in second ch from hook. (*2 sts*)
Row 2: 1ch (does not count as st throughout), 2sc in each st. (*4 sts*)
Row 3: 1ch, 2sc in first st, 1sc in next st, 2sc in next st, 1sc in last st. (*6 sts*)
Row 4: 1ch, 2sc in first st, 1sc in each of next 2 sts, 2sc in next st, 1sc in each of last 2 sts. (*8 sts*)
Cut A, do not fasten off.
Row 5: Join B, 1ch, 1sc in each st to end. (*8 sts*)
Row 6: 1ch, 2sc in first st, 1sc in each of next 3 sts, 2sc in next st, 1sc in each of last 3 sts. (*10 sts*)
Row 7: 1ch, 2sc in first st, 1sc in each of next 4 sts, 2sc in next st, 1sc in each of last 4 sts. (*12 sts*)
Row 8: 1ch, 2sc in first st, 1sc in each of next 5 sts, 2sc in next st, 1sc in each of last 5 sts. (*14 sts*)
Cut yarn, do not fasten off.
Row 9: Join A, 1ch, 2sc in first st, 1sc in each of next 6 sts, 2sc in next st, 1sc in each of last 6 sts. (*16 sts*)
Row 10: 1ch, 1sc in each st to end. (*16 sts*)
Row 11: 1ch, 2sc in first st, 1sc in each of next 7 sts, 2sc in next st, 1sc in each of last 7 sts. (*18 sts*)
Fasten off.

Press both pieces flat.

Place st marker in center edge along bottom edge of Hat.
With RS of two pieces of Face facing, center and pin Face onto front of Hat starting at bottom edge leaving approx 3 sts apart at bottom edge. Sew Face pieces to front of Hat using MC at bottom and straight central edge by sewing running stitch from WS of Hat, and A around curved edges using overcast stitch.

Eyes

Using A and B, embroider eyes in satin stitch (see page 18) onto Face on black section, embroidering A first, then B on top of A.

Nose

Work in rounds, placing st marker at beg of each round.
Round 1: Using B and 5mm (US size H/8) hook, make 2ch, 6sc in second ch from hook. (6 sts)
Round 2: 2sc in each st to end. (12 sts)
Round 3: *1sc in next st, 2sc in next st; rep from * to end. (18 sts)
Rounds 4–5: 1sc in each st to end. (18 sts)
Ss in next st. Fasten off leaving a long tail for sewing on.
Lightly stuff the Nose using the ends from yarn B.
Pin Nose to bottom edge of center of Face and sew in place.

Inner ear

(make 2)
Row 1: Using A and US size E/4 (3.5mm) hook, 2ch, 3sc in second ch from hook. (3 sts)
Row 2: 1ch, 2sc in first st, 1sc in next st, 2sc in last st. (5 sts)
Row 3: 1ch, 1sc in each st to end. (5 sts)
Row 4: 1ch, 2sc in first st, 1sc in each of next 3 sts, 2sc in last st. (7 sts)
Row 5: 1ch, 1sc in each st to end. (7 sts)
Row 6: 1ch, 2sc in first st, 1sc in each of next 5 sts, 2sc in last st. (9 sts)
Row 7: 1ch, 2sc in first st, 1sc in each of next 7 sts, 2sc in last st. (11 sts)
Rows 8–10: 1ch, 1sc in each st to end. (11 sts)
Fasten off inner ear.

Outer Ear

(make 2)
Using B and US size E/4 (3.5mm) hook, rep Rows 1–10 of Inner ear.

Do not fasten off Outer ear, pull up loop so work doesn't unravel and take hook out of loop.

Sew in ends.
With RS of Outer and WS of Inner facing, pin Inner and Outer ears together.

Pick up loop by inserting hook again and pull yarn to tighten loop onto hook. 1ch, sc 9 sts around each of next two edges of both ears, leaving bottom edge of both pieces open and making 3sc in tip. Fasten off.

Sew Ears onto Hat using MC, with Ears curved slightly forward and with Inner ears facing to front.

Frankie the frog

How can this fail to make you smile? A mossy green yarn makes this Frog really stand out.

Materials

Fyberspates Scrumptious Aran, 55% merino wool, 45% silk worsted (aran) yarn, 100g (3½oz) hank, approx 180yd (165m) per hank:
   1 x hank of shade 402 Moss (MC)

Debbie Bliss Cashmerino Aran, 55% merino wool, 33% acrylic, 12% cashmere worsted (aran) yarn, 1¾oz (50g) balls, approx 98yd (90m) per ball:
   1 x ball of shade 025 White (A)

Small amount of black bulky (chunky) yarn (B)

US size H/8 (5mm) crochet hook

Yarn sewing needle

Gauge

15 sts x 11 rows over a 4in square using US size H/8 (5mm) hook, half double crochet, and Scrumptious Aran.

Size

To fit age 6–24 months

Finished measurements

Approx 16–18in (40.5–46cm) circumference, 6½in (16.5cm) high

Abbreviations

approx approximately
beg beginning
ch chain
hdc half double crochet
sc single crochet
sc2tog single crochet 2 stitches together
rep repeat
ss slip stitch
st(s) stitch(es)

Hat

Work in rounds, placing st marker at beg of each round.

Round 1: Using MC, 2ch, 8hdc in second ch from hook. *(8 sts)*
Round 2: 2hdc in each st. *(16 sts)*
Round 3: *1hdc in next st, 2hdc in next st; rep from * to end. *(24 sts)*
Round 4: *1hdc in each of next 2 sts, 2hdc in next st; rep from * to end. *(32 sts)*
Round 5: *1hdc in each of next 3 sts, 2hdc in next st; rep from * to end. *(40 sts)*
Round 6: *1hdc in each of next 4 sts, 2hdc in next st; rep from * to end. *(48 sts)*
Round 7: *1hdc in each of next 5 sts, 2hdc in next st; rep from * to end. *(56 sts)*
Round 8: *1hdc in each of next 6 sts, 2hdc in next st; rep from * to end. *(64 sts)*
Rounds 9–19: 1hdc in each st to end. *(64 sts)* or until work measures approx 6½in (16.5cm) from start.
Next round: 1sc in each st, ss in last st.
Fasten off.

Using B, embroider the mouth using backstitch, using the photo as a guide.

Outer eyes

(make two)

Work in rounds, placing st marker at beg of each round.

Round 1: Using MC, make 2ch, 8sc in second ch from hook. *(8 sts)*

Round 2: 2sc in each st to end. *(16 sts)*

Round 3: *1sc in each of next 2 sts, 2sc in next st; rep from * to last st, 1sc in last st. *(21 sts)*

Rounds 4–6: 1sc in each st to end. *(21 sts)*

Round 7: *1sc in each of next 2 sts, sc2tog; rep from * to last st, 1sc in last st. *(16 sts)*

Round 8: *1sc in each of next 3 sts, sc2tog; rep from * to last st, 1sc in last st. *(13 sts)*

Ss in next st.

Fasten off, leaving a long tail for sewing on.

Inner eyes

(make 2)

Work in rounds, placing st marker at beg of each round.

Round 1: Using A, 2ch, 6sc in second ch from hook. *(6 sts)*

Round 2: 2sc in each st. *(12 sts)*

Round 3: *1sc in next st, 2sc in next st; rep from * to end. *(18 sts)*

Ss in next st.

Fasten off.

Center Inner eyes onto Outer eyes and sew around edges. Using B, embroider pupils in satin stitch (see page 18) in center of each of Inner eyes.

Place Eyes approx 1in (2.5cm) apart at top of Hat and sew in place.

Marcel the monkey

The smile on this cute hat makes it a perfect gift for the cheeky monkey in your life.

Materials
Debbie Bliss Rialto DK, 100% merino wool light worsted (DK) yarn, 1¾oz (50g) balls, approx 115yd (105m) per ball:
- 1 x ball of shade 05 Chocolate (brown) (MC)
- 1 x ball of shade 06 Stone (beige) (A)

Small amount of black bulky (chunky) yarn (B)

Small amount of black light worsted (DK) yarn (C)

US size E/4 (3.5mm) crochet hook

Small amount of polyester toy stuffing

Gauge
20 sts x 22 rows over a 4in (10cm) square using US size E/4 (3.5mm) hook, single crochet, and Rialto DK.

Size
To fit age 6–24 months

Finished measurements
Approx 16–18in 40.5–46cm) circumference, 6½in (16.5cm) high

Abbreviations
approx approximately
beg begin(ning)
ch chain
dc double crochet
hdc half double crochet
rep repeat
RS right side
sc single crochet
ss slip stitch
st(s) stitch(es)
WS wrong side

Hat
Work in rounds, placing st marker at beg of each round.
Round 1: Using MC, 2ch, 6sc in second ch from hook. (6 sts)
Round 2: 2sc in each st to end. (12 sts)
Round 3: *1sc in next st, 2sc in next st; rep from * to end. (18 sts)
Round 4: *1sc in each of next 2 sts, 2sc in next st; rep from * to end. (24 sts)
Round 5: *1sc in each of next 3 sts, 2sc in next st; rep from * to end. (30 sts)
Round 6: *1sc in each of next 4 sts, 2sc in next st; rep from * to end. (36 sts)
Round 7: *1sc in each of next 5 sts, 2sc in next st; rep from * to end. (42 sts)
Round 8: *1sc in each of next 6 sts, 2sc in next st; rep from * to end. (48 sts)
Round 9: *1sc in each of next 7 sts, 2sc in next st; rep from * to end. (54 sts)
Round 10: *1sc in each of next 8 sts, 2sc in next st; rep from * to end. (60 sts)
Round 11: *1sc in each of next 9 sts, 2sc in next st; rep from * to end. (66 sts)
Round 12: *1sc in each of next 10 sts, 2sc in next st; rep from * to end. (72 sts)
Rounds 13–36: 1sc in each st to end. (72 sts)
Do not fasten off.

First earflap:
1sc in each of next 6 sts. Do not turn.
Beg working in rows, turning at end of each following row.
Row 1 (RS): 1sc in each of next 15 sts. Turn. (15 sts)
Row 2 (WS): 1ch, sc2tog,1sc in each of next 11 sts, sc2tog. (13 sts)
Row 3: 1ch, 1sc in each st to end. (13 sts)
Row 4: 1ch, sc2tog, 1sc in each of next 9 sts, sc2tog. (11 sts)
Row 5: 1ch, 1sc in each st to end. (11 sts)
Row 6: 1ch, sc2tog, 1sc in each of next 7 sts, sc2tog. (9 sts)
Row 7: 1ch, 1sc in each st to end. (9 sts)
Row 8: 1ch, sc2tog, 1sc in each of next 5 sts, sc2tog. (7 sts)
Row 9: 1ch, 1sc in each st to end. (7 sts)
Row 10: 1ch, sc2tog, 1sc in each of next 3 sts, sc2tog. (5 sts)
Row 11: 1ch, 1sc in each st to end. (5 sts)
Row 12: 1ch, sc2tog, 1sc in next st, sc2tog. (3 sts)
Rows 13–14: 1ch, 1sc in each st to end. (3 sts)
Fasten off.

Second earflap:
With RS facing, join MC in next st along from end of Row 1 of First earflap.
1ch, 1sc in same st, 1sc in each of next 11 sts, place second st marker here to denote center front of Hat, 1sc in each of next 12 sts. Do not turn. (24 sts)
Work in rows, turning at end of each following row.
Row 1: 1sc in each of next 15 sts. Turn.
Rep Rows 2–14 of First earflap.

Tips

It's important to have the correct amount of stitches at the end of the first round of the Muzzle, so count stitches carefully. Insert a stitch marker in first stitch of each round. The last stitch of the round is the stitch with the stitch marker.

In Rounds 2, 3, 4 and 5, the 3hdcs are always made in the center stitch of the 3hdc from the previous round.

Edging:

With RS of work facing, rejoin MC at back of work at start of straight edging after Earflap.

1ch, 1sc in same st, 1sc in each of next 17 sts along back of Hat to start of Earflap.

Make 12 sc evenly down first edge of first Earflap.

2sc in first of 3 sts at bottom edge, 1sc in next st, 2sc in next st, make 12 sc evenly along other edge of Earflap, 1sc in each of next 24 sts along front of Hat, make 12 sc evenly along first edge of next Earflap; rep from ** to **, join with a ss in first sc. *(100 sts)*
Fasten off.

Eye backs with Eye Sockets

Row 1: Using A, make 2ch, 3sc in second ch from hook, turn.
Row 2: 1ch, 2sc in each st. *(6 sts)*
Row 3: 1ch, 2sc in first st, 1sc in next st, 2hdc in each of next 2 sts, 1sc in next st, 2sc in last st. *(10 sts)*
Row 4: 1ch, 2sc in first st, 1sc in next st, 2hdc in each of next 6 sts, 1sc in next st, 2sc in last st. *(18 sts)*
Row 5: 1ch, 1sc in each of first 4 sts, 1hdc in next st, 2hdc in each of next 8 sts, 1hdc in next st, 1sc in each of last 4 sts. *(26 sts)*
Fasten off.

Using B, embroider pupils in satin stitch (see page 18), using the photo as a guide.

Muzzle

Round 1: Using A, make 12ch (foundation chain), 1hdc in second ch from hook, 1hdc in each of next 9 ch, 3hdc in last ch.
Working on underside of foundation chain, 1hdc in each of next 10 ch, 3hdc in first foundation chain. *(26 sts)*
Round 2: 1hdc in each of next 11 sts, 3hdc in next st (center st of 3-dc from previous round), 1hdc in each of next 12 sts, 3hdc in next st, 1hdc in last st. *(30 sts)*
Round 3: 1hdc in each of next 12 sts, 3hdc in next st, 1hdc in each of next 14 sts, 3hdc in next st, 1hdc in each of last 2 sts. *(34 sts)*
Round 4: 1hdc in each of next 13 sts, 3hdc in next st, 1hdc in each of next 16 sts, 3hdc in next st, 1hdc in each of last 3 sts. *(38 sts)*
Round 5: 1hdc in each of next 14 sts, 3hdc in next st, 1hdc in each of next 18 sts, 3hdc in next st, 1hdc in each of last 4 sts. *(42 sts)*
Ss in next st, fasten off leaving a long tail for sewing on.

Insert st marker in bottom edge on Muzzle to mark center.
Using MC, embroider mouth onto Muzzle using backstitch.

Match up st markers on center front of Hat and on center of Muzzle. Pin and sew Muzzle to front of Hat, with Muzzle bottom edge approx 2 rows up from bottom edge of Hat. Leave a small gap, stuff muzzle, finish sewing gap.

Place st marker in top center of Muzzle as guide to place eyes.

Place eyes with RS facing and matching bottom corners to st marker at center of Muzzle. Pin and sew eyes onto Hat by sewing bottom edge of eyes (straight edge) to top edge of Muzzle first, then sew rest of eye (curved edge) onto Hat.

Nostrils

Using C, 2ch, 1dc in second ch from hook, 1ch, ss in same place, 1ch, 1dc in same place, 1ch, ss in same place.
Fasten off.

Sew Nostrils between eyes at top of Muzzle.

Ears

(make 2 in A for Inner, 2 in MC for Outer)
Work in rows, turning at end of row.
Row 1: 2ch, 7sc in second ch from hook. Turn.
Row 2: 1ch, 1sc in first st, 2sc in next st, 1sc in each of next 3 sts, 2sc in next st, 1sc in last st. *(9 sts)*
Row 3: 1ch, 1sc in each of next 3 sts, 2sc in each of next 3 sts, 1sc in each of last 3 sts. *(12 sts)*
Fasten off.

Place one Inner and Outer WS together. Join MC at bottom edge, 1ch. Working through both pieces, make 1sc in each st around top edge. Make 3sc evenly along first half of bottom edge (straight edge) to center, 1sc in center, 3sc evenly along second half of bottom edge, join with a ss in first sc.
Fasten off leaving a long tail for sewing onto Hat.

Rep with other inner and outer.
Sew Ears in place on sides of Hat with top of Ears in line with top of Eyes at approx 6in (15cm) apart with RS (inner ear) facing to front. Sew in ends.

A lovely quick project that took me around six hours to make in total, so it can be made over a couple of evenings. The main hat is crocheted in half double crochet and the eyes and nose in single crochet.

Amanda the baby panda

Materials
Debbie Bliss Cashmerino Aran, 55% merino wool, 33% acrylic, 12% cashmere worsted (aran) yarn, 1¾oz (50g) balls, approx 98yd (90m) per ball:
    1 x ball of shade 025 White (MC)
    1 x ball of shade 300 Black (A)

Small amount of black bulky (chunky) yarn for eyes (B)

US size H/8 (5mm) and US size E/4 (3.5mm) crochet hooks

Yarn sewing needle

Small amount of polyester toy stuffing

Gauge
15 sts x 11 rows over a 4in (10cm) square using US size H/8 (5mm) hook, half double crochet, and Cashmerino Aran.

Size
To fit age 6–24 months

Finished measurements
Approx 16-18in (40.5–46cm) circumference, 6½in (16.5cm) high

Abbreviationsv
approx approximately
beg begin(ning)
ch chain
hdc half double crochet
rep repeat
sc single crochet
ss slip stitch
st(s) stitch(es)

Hat
Work in rounds, placing st marker at beg of each round.
Round 1: Using MC and US size H/8 (5mm) hook, 2ch, 6hdc in second ch from hook. (*6 sts*)
Rounds 2–3: 2hdc in each st. (*24 sts*)
Round 4: *1hdc in each of next 2 sts, 2hdc in next st; rep from * to end. (*32 sts*)
Round 5: *1hdc in each of next 3 sts, 2hdc in next st; rep from * to end. (*40 sts*)
Round 6: *1hdc in each of next 4 sts, 2hdc in next st; rep from * to end. (*48 sts*)
Round 7: *1hdc in each of next 5 sts, 2hdc in next st; rep from * to end. (*56 sts*)
Round 8: *1hdc in each of next 6 sts, 2hdc in next st; rep from * to end. (*64 sts*)
Rounds 9–19: 1hdc in each st to end, or until work measures approx 6½in (16.5cm) from start. (*64 sts*)
Cut yarn, join A.
Next round: 1sc in each st, ss in last st.
Fasten off.

Muzzle

Work in rounds, placing st marker at beg of each round.

Round 1: Using MC and US size E/4 (3.5mm) hook, make 2ch, 6sc in second ch from hook. *(6 sts)*

Round 2: 2sc in each st to end. *(12 sts)*

Round 3: *1sc in next st, 2sc in next st; rep from * to end. *(18 sts)*

Round 4: *1sc in each of next 2 sts, 2sc in next st; rep from * to end. *(24 sts)*

Rounds 5–7: 1sc in each st to end. *(24 sts)*

Ss in next st.

Fasten off leaving a long tail for sewing on.

Center Muzzle at front of Hat approx 1 row up from bottom edge. Leave small gap before stuffing lightly. Continue to close gap and sew in end.

Nose

Work in rows, turning at end of row.

Row 1: Using B and US size E/4 (3.5mm) hook, make 2ch, 3sc in second ch from hook. *(3 sts)*

Row 2: 1ch (does not count as st throughout), 1sc in each st. *(3 sts)*

Row 3: 1ch, 2sc in next st, 1sc in next st, 2sc in next st. *(5 sts)*

Row 4: 1ch, 1sc in each st.

Fasten off leaving a long tail for sewing on.

Sew in ends carefully, at same time neatening up triangle shape. Sew Nose onto center of Muzzle with point facing downward and add straight stitches (see page 18) for the mouth, using the photo as a guide.

Eyes

(make two)

Round 1: Using B and US size E/4 (3.5mm) hook, make 2ch, 6sc in second ch from hook. *(6 sts)*

Round 2: 2sc in each st. Cut yarn. *(12 sts)*

Round 3: Join MC, *1sc in next st, 2sc in next st. *(18 sts)*

Round 4: *1sc in each of next 2 sts, 2sc in next st. *(24 sts)*

Ss in next st.

Fasten off.

Position Eyes onto Hat approx 7 sts apart and 6 rows up from the bottom of Hat.

Using B, embroider pupil in satin stitch (see page 18) in center of each Eye, using the photo as a guide.

Ears

(make 2)

Work in rounds, placing st marker at beg of each round.

Using A and US size E/4 (3.5mm) hook, make 2ch, 6sc in second ch from hook.

Round 1: 2sc in each st to end. *(12 sts)*

Round 2: *1sc in each of next 2 sts, 2sc in next st; rep from * to end. *(16 sts)*

Round 3: *1sc in each of next 3 sts, 2sc in next st; rep from * to end. *(20 sts)*

Rounds 4–6: 1sc in each st to end.

Ss in next st.

Fasten off leaving a long tail for sewing on.

Sew in end from starting point.

Sew on Ears at center top of hat approx 3in (7.5cm) apart.

Thor the penguin

A very distinctive hat, that is just perfect for a little one.

Materials

Debbie Bliss Cashmerino Aran, 55% merino wool, 33% acrylic, 12% cashmere worsted (aran) yarn, 1¾oz (50g) balls, approx 98yd (90m) per ball:
- 1 x ball of shade 300 Black (MC)
- 1 x ball of shade 025 White (A)

Debbie Bliss Baby Cashmerino, 55% wool, 33% acrylic, 12% cashmere sportweight (4ply) yarn, 1¾oz (50g) balls, approx 137yd (125m) per ball:
- 1 x ball of shade 092 Orange (B)

Small amount of black bulky (chunky) yarn for eyes (C)

US size H/8 (5mm) and US size E/4 (3.5mm) crochet hooks

Gauge

15 sts x 11 rows over a 4in (10cm) square using US size H/8 (5mm) hook, half double crochet, and Cashmerino Aran.

Size

To fit age 6–24 months

Finished measurements

Approx 16–18in (40.5–46cm) circumference, 6½in (16.5cm) high

Abbreviations

approx approximately
beg beginning
ch chain
dc double crochet
hdc half double crochet
rep repeat
RS right side
sc single crochet
sc2tog single crochet 2 stitches together
ss slip stitch
st(s) stitch(es)
WS wrong side

Hat

Work in rounds, placing st marker at beg of each round.

Round 1: Using MC and US size H/8 (5mm) hook, 2ch, 8hdc in second ch from hook. (*8 sts*)

Round 2: 2hdc in each st. (*16 sts*)

Round 3: *1hdc in next st, 2hdc in next st; rep from * to end. (*24 sts*)

Round 4: *1hdc in each of next 2 sts, 2hdc in next st; rep from * to end. (*32 sts*)

Round 5: *1hdc in each of next 3 sts, 2hdc in next st; rep from * to end. (*40 sts*)

Round 6: *1hdc in each of next 4 sts, 2hdc in next st; rep from * to end. (*48 sts*)

Round 7: *1hdc in each of next 5 sts, 2hdc in next st; rep from * to end. (*56 sts*)

Round 8: *1hdc in each of next 6 sts, 2hdc in next st; rep from * to end. (*64 sts*)

Rounds 9–19: 1hdc in each st to end, or until work measures approx 6½in (16.5cm). (*64 sts*)

Next round: 1sc in each st, ss in last st. Fasten off.

Face

Work in rows, turning at the end of each row.

Row 1 (RS): Using A and US size H/8 (5mm) hook, 2ch, 3sc in second ch from hook. (*3 sts*)

Row 2: 1ch, 2sc in each st. (*6 sts*)

Row 3: 1ch, *1sc in next st, 2sc in next st; rep from * to end. (*9 sts*)

Row 4: 1ch, *1sc in each of next 2 sts, 2sc in next st; rep from * to end. (*12 sts*)

Row 5: 1ch, *1sc in each of next 3 sts, 2sc in next st; rep from * to end. (*15 sts*)

Row 6: 1ch, *1sc in each of next 4 sts, 2sc in next st; rep from * to end. (*18 sts*)

Row 7: 1ch, *1sc in each of next 5 sts, 2sc in next st; rep from * to end. (*21 sts*)

Row 8: 1ch, *1sc in each of next 6 sts, 2sc in next st; rep from * to end. (*24 sts*)

Row 9: 1ch, *1sc in each of next 7 sts, 2sc in next st; rep from * to end. (*27 sts*)

Row 10: 1ch, *1sc in each of next 8 sts, 2sc in next st; rep from * to end. (*30 sts*)

Row 11: 1ch, 1sc in each of next 4 sts, 1hdc in each of next 2 sts, 1dc in each of next 4 sts, 1hdc in each of next 4 sts, 1sc in each of next 2 sts, 1hdc in each of next 4 sts, 1dc in each of next 4 sts, 1hdc in each of next 2 sts, 1sc in each of next 4 sts. (*30 sts*)

Row 12: 1ch, 1sc in each of next 3 sts, 1hdc in each of next 2 sts, 1dc in next st, 2 dc in each of next 4 sts, 1dc in each of next 2 sts, 1hdc in each of next 2 sts, sc2tog, 1hdc in each of next 2 sts, 1dc in each of next 2 sts, 2dc in each of next 4 sts, 1dc in next st, 1hdc in each of next 2 sts, 1sc in each of next 3 sts. (*37 sts*).

Do not fasten off.

Edging RS:

Continue with A. Turn and work along bottom of Face (straight edge). 1ch, make 25 sc evenly along bottom edge.

Fasten off, leaving a long tail for sewing on.

Center Face on front of Hat, with straight edge of Face along bottom edge of Hat. Pin and sew using long tail.

Eyes

Using C, embroider eyes in satin stitch (see page 18) using the photo as a guide.

Beak

Work in rounds, placing st marker at beg of each round.

Round 1: Using B and US size E/4 (3.5mm) hook, make 2ch, 6sc

Tips

When sewing on small pieces such as the Nose, use a yarn sewing needle with a sharp end.

When fastening off face details, leave ends long for sewing them onto the hat.

in second ch from hook.

Round 2: 2sc in each st. (*12 sts*)

Rounds 3–6: 1sc in each st.

Fasten off, leaving a long tail.

Using yarn end from start of Beak, weave around stitches to close hole in Round 1.

Use long tail to sew Beak onto Face approx 3 rows from top edge.

A lovely bright hat for a baby or toddler—and the wobbly antennae make it even cuter.

Lulu the ladybug

Materials

Debbie Bliss Rialto DK, 100% merino wool light worsted (DK) yarn, 1¾oz (50g) balls, approx 115yd (105m) per ball:

   1 x ball of shade 012 Scarlet (MC)
   1 x ball of shade 003 Black (A)

US size E/4 (3.5mm) crochet hook

Gauge

20 sts x 22 rows over a 4in (10cm) square using US size E/4 (3.5mm) hook, single crochet, and Rialto DK.

Size

To fit age 6–24 months

Finished measurements

Approx 16–18in (40.5–46cm) circumference, 6½in (16.5cm) high

Abbreviations

approx approximately
beg begin(ning)
ch chain
rep repeat
RS right side
sc single crochet
ss slip stitch
st(s) stitch(es)
WS wrong side

Hat

Work in rounds, placing st marker at beg of each round.

Round 1: Using MC, 2ch, 6sc in second ch from hook. (*6 sts*)

Round 2: 2sc in each st to end. (*12 sts*)

Round 3: *1sc in next st, 2sc in next st; rep from * to end. (*18 sts*)

Round 4: *1sc in each of next 2 sts, 2sc in next st; rep from * to end. (*24 sts*)

Round 5: *1sc in each of next 3 sts, 2sc in next st; rep from * to end. (*30 sts*)

Round 6: *1sc in each of next 4 sts, 2sc in next st; rep from * to end. (*36 sts*)

Round 7: *1sc in each of next 5 sts, 2sc in next st; rep from * to end. (*42 sts*)

Round 8: *1sc in each of next 6 sts, 2sc in next st; rep from * to end. (*48 sts*)

Round 9: *1sc in each of next 7 sts, 2sc in next st; rep from * to end. (*54 sts*)

Round 10: *1sc in each of next 8 sts, 2sc in next st; rep from * to end. (*60 sts*)

Round 11: *1sc in each of next 9 sts, 2sc in next st; rep from * to end. (*66 sts*)

Round 12: *1sc in each of next 10 sts, 2sc in next st; rep from * to end. (*72 sts*)

Round 13: *1sc in each of next 11 sts, 2sc in next st; rep from * to end. (*78 sts*)

Round 14: *1sc in each of next 12 sts, 2sc in next st; rep form * to end. (*84 sts*)

Rounds 15–36: 1sc in each st to end. (*84 sts*)

Ss in next st. Fasten off.

Spots

(*make seven*)

Round 1: Using A, make 2ch, 6sc in second ch from hook. (*6 sts*)

Round 2: 2sc in each st to end. (*12 sts*)

Round 3: *1sc in next st, 2sc in next st; rep from * to end. (*18 sts*)

Ss in next st and fasten off leaving a long tail for sewing onto Hat.

Press all Spots with a damp cloth on WS.
Sew Spots on Front and Back of Hat.

Antennae

(*make two*)

Working on RS throughout.

Round 1: Using A, 2ch, 6sc in second ch from hook. (*6 sts*)

Round 2: 2sc in each st. (*12 sts*)

Round 3: 1sc in each st to end. (*12 sts*)

Round 4: *1sc in next st, sc2tog; rep from * to end. (*8 sts*)

Sew in end on WS and continue to work on RS.

Rounds 5–11: 1sc in each st to end. (*8 sts*)

Ss in next st, fasten off.

Sew Antenna 3in (7.5cm) apart, starting seven rounds from top center of Hat.

Pearl the pig

This hat is for all the pig fanatics out there. When embroidering the eyes, make sure you keep them small and "pig-like".

Materials

Debbie Bliss Cashmerino Aran, 55% merino wool, 33% acrylic, 12% cashmere worsted (aran) yarn, 1¾oz (50g) balls, approx 98yd (90m) per ball:

    1 x ball of shade 603 Baby Pink (pink) (MC):

Scrap of black bulky (chunky) yarn

US size H/8 (5mm) and US size E/4 (3.5mm) crochet hooks

Yarn sewing needle

Gauge

15 sts x 11 rows over a 4in (10cm) square using US size H/8 (5mm) hook, half double crochet, and Cashmerino Aran.

Size

To fit age 6–24 months

Finished measurements

Approx 16–18in (40.5–46cm) circumference, 6½in (16.5cm) high

Abbreviations

approx approximately
beg begin(ning)
ch chain
dc double crochet
hdc half double crochet
rep repeat
sc single crochet
sc2tog single crochet 2 stitches together
ss slip stitch
st(s) stitch(es)

Hat

Work in rounds, placing st marker at beg of each round.

Round 1: Using MC and US size H/8 (5mm) hook, 2ch, 8hdc in second ch from hook. *(8 sts)*

Round 2: 2hdc in each st. *(16 sts)*

Round 3: *1hdc in next st, 2hdc in next st; rep from * to end. *(24 sts)*

Round 4: *1hdc in each of next 2 sts, 2hdc in next st; rep from * to end. *(32 sts)*

Round 5: *1hdc in each of next 3 sts, 2hdc in next st; rep from * to end. *(40 sts)*

Round 6: *1hdc in each of next 4 sts, 2hdc in next st; rep from * to end. *(48 sts)*

Round 7: *1hdc in each of next 5 sts, 2hdc in next st; rep from * to end. *(56 sts)*

Round 8: *1hdc in each of next 6 sts, 2hdc in next st; rep from * to end. *(64 sts)*

Rounds 9–19: 1hdc in each st to end, or until work measures approx 6½in (16.5cm) from start. *(64 sts)*

Next round: 1sc in each st, ss in last st.
Fasten off.

Nose

Round 1: Using MC and US size E/4 (3.5mm) hook, 2ch, 6sc in second ch from hook *(6 sts)*.

Round 2: 2sc in each st to end. *(12 sts)*

Round 3: *1sc in next st, 2sc in next st, rep from * to end. *(18 sts)*

Round 4: *1sc in each of next 2 sts, 2sc in next st; rep from * to end. *(24 sts)*

Round 5: *1sc in each of next 3 sts, 2sc in next st; rep from * to end. *(30 sts)*

Round 6: *1sc in each of next 4 sts, 2sc in next st; rep from * to end. *(36 sts)*

Rounds 7–9: 1sc in each st to end. *(36 sts)*
Ss in next st. Fasten off.

Sew Nose to front of Hat approx one row from bottom edge. Leave a gap and stuff Nose, sew gap closed.

Ears

(make 2)

Row 1: Using MC and US size H/8 (5mm) hook, 3ch, 2sc in second ch from hook, 2sc in last ch. *(4 sts)*

Row 2: 1ch (does not count as st throughout), 2sc in first st, 1sc in each of next 2 sts, 2sc in last st. *(6 sts)*

Row 3: 1ch, 1sc in each st to end. *(6 sts)*

Row 4: 1ch, 2sc in first st, 1sc in each of next 4 sts, 2sc in last st. *(8 sts)*

Row 5: 1ch, 1sc in each st to end. *(8 sts)*

Row 6: 1ch, 2sc in first st, 1sc in each of next 6 sts, 2sc in last st. *(10 sts)*

Rows 7–9: 1ch, 1sc in each st to end. *(10 sts)*

Row 10: 1ch, sc2tog, 1sc in each of next 6 sts, sc2tog. *(8 sts)*

Rows 11–13: 1ch, 1sc in each st to end. *(8 sts)*
Fasten off.

Press Ears flat.
Sew Ears to top of head, starting approx one row down from center.

Sew in ends.
Using black yarn and French knots (see page 19), embroider eyes approx eight rows from bottom edge and eight sts apart. Embroider nostrils in satin stitch (see page 18) on Nose approx 4 rows up from center of Nose and 4 sts apart.

A popular and favorite animal with many children. This project has a lot of detail, what with all the spots, horns, nose, and eyes. Make sure you put a stitch marker to denote the center front of the hat when sewing on the pieces—have fun with this, and add your own embellishments, too.

Jackie the giraffe

Materials
Debbie Bliss Cashmerino Aran, 55% merino wool, 33% acrylic, 12% cashmere worsted (aran) yarn, 1¾oz (50g) balls, approx 98yd (90m) per ball
　　1 x ball of shade 077 Gold (yellow) (A)
　　1 x ball of shade 066 Mustard (light brown) (B)

Small amount of black bulky (chunky) yarn for eyes, nostrils and eyelashes

US size H/8 (5mm) and US size E/4 (3.5mm) crochet hooks

Yarn sewing needle

Small amount of polyester toy stuffing

Gauge
15 sts x 11 rows over a 4in (10cm) square using US size H/8 (5mm) hook, half double crochet, and Cashmerino Aran.

Size
To fit age 6–24 months

Finished measurements
Approx 16–18in (40.5–46cm) circumference, 6½in (16.5cm) high

Abbreviations
approx approximately
beg beginning
ch chain
dc double crochet
hdc half double crochet
rep repeat
RS right side
sc single crochet
sc2tog single crochet 2 stitches together
ss slip stitch
st(s) stitch(es)
WS wrong side

Hat
Work in rounds, placing st marker at beg of each round.
Round 1: Using A and US size H/8 (5mm) hook, 2ch, 8hdc in second ch from hook. (*8 sts*)
Round 2: 2hdc in each st. (*16 sts*)
Round 3: *1hdc in next st, 2hdc in next st; rep from * to end. (*24 sts*)
Round 4: *1hdc in each of next 2 sts, 2hdc in next st; rep from * to end. (*32 sts*)
Round 5: *1hdc in each of next 3 sts, 2hdc in next st; rep from * to end. (*40 sts*)

Round 6: *1hdc in each of next 4 sts, 2hdc in next st; rep from * to end. (*48 sts*)
Round 7: *1hdc in each of next 5 sts, 2hdc in next st; rep from * to end. (*56 sts*)
Round 8: *1hdc in each of next 6 sts, 2hdc in next st; rep from * to end. (*64 sts*)
Rounds 9–19: 1hdc in each st to end, until hat measures approx 6½in (16.5cm). (*64 sts*)
Next round: 1sc in each st to end, ss in last st. Fasten off.

Ears

(make 2)

Round 1: Using A and US size H/8 (5mm) hook, 2ch, 4sc in second ch from hook. *(4 sts)*

Round 2: 2sc in each st to end. *(8 sts)*

Round 3: *1sc in each of next 3 sts, 2sc in next st; rep from * to end. *(10 sts)*

Round 4: *1sc in each of next 4 sts, 2sc in next st; rep from * to end. *(12 sts)*

Round 5: *1sc in each of next 5 sts, 2sc in next st; rep from * to end. *(14 sts)*

Round 6: *1sc in each of next 6 sts, 2sc in next st; rep from * to end. *(16 sts)*

Round 7: *1sc in each of next 7 sts, 2sc in next st; rep from * to end. *(18 sts)*

Round 8: *1sc in each of next 8 sts, 2sc in next st; rep from * to end. *(20 sts)*

Rounds 9–12: 1sc in each st to end. *(20 sts)*

Ss in next st.

Fasten off leaving a long tail for sewing on.

Horns

(make two)

Work on RS throughout.

Round 1: Using B and US size E/4 (3.5mm) hook, 2ch, 6sc in second ch from hook. *(6 sts)*

Round 2: 2sc in each st. *(12 sts)*

Round 3: *1sc in each of next 2 sts, 2sc in next st; rep from * to end. *(16 sts)*

Round 4: 1sc in each st to end. *(16 sts)*

Round 5: *1sc in each of next 2 sts, sc2tog; rep from * to end. *(12 sts)*

Round 6: Rep Round 5. Cut yarn, do not fasten off. *(9 sts)*

Rounds 7–11: Join A, 1sc in each st to end. *(9 sts)*

Ss in next st, fasten off.

Sew each Horn on Hat approx 1½in (4cm) apart starting 2 rows down from top of Hat. Sew Ears on Hat approx 3½in (9cm) apart starting 4 rows down from top of Hat.

Tip

To help with sewing up, sew Horns onto Hat after sewing Ears.

Muzzle

Work in rounds, placing st marker at beg of each round.

Round 1: Using B and US size E/4 (3.5mm) hook, make 2ch, 6sc in second ch from hook. (*6 sts*)

Round 2: 2sc in each st to end. (*12 sts*)

Round 3: *1sc in next st, 2sc in next st; rep from * to end. (*18 sts*)

Round 4: *1sc in each of next 2 sts, 2sc in next st; rep from * to end. (*24 sts*)

Round 5: *1sc in each of next 3 sts, 2sc in next st; rep from * to end. (*30 sts*)

Round 6: *1sc in each of next 4 sts, 2sc in next st; rep from * to end. (*36 sts*)

Rounds 7–11: 1sc in each st to end. (*36 sts*)

Ss in next st.

Fasten off leaving a long tail for sewing on.

Center Muzzle approx one row up from bottom edge. Leave small gap before stuffing lightly. Continue to close gap and sew in end.

Using black yarn, embroider nostrils in satin stitch (see page 18) and mouth in backstitch.

Using black yarn, embroider eyes and eyelashes approx 8 sts apart and 2 rows above Muzzle.

Tail

Round 1: Using A and US size E/4 (3.5mm) hook, make 2ch, leaving a long tail, 6sc in second ch from hook. (*6 sts*)

Round 2: 1sc in each st around, until work measures approx 3in (7.5cm). Fasten off leaving a long tail.

Using this yarn end, weave around sts and pull tight to close hole.

Using B, cut approx 5 strands of yarn approx 5in (12.5cm) long. Thread all strands through closed end of Tail to create small tassel. Trim tassel end.

Using yarn end at open end of Tail, sew onto back of Hat approx four rows from bottom edge.

Spots

(*make 3 large and 1 small*)

All spots:

Round 1: Using B and US size E/4 (3.5mm) hook, make 2ch, 6sc in second ch from hook. (*6 sts*)

Round 2: 2sc in each st to end. (*12 sts*)

Round 3: *1sc in next st, 2sc in next st; rep from * to end. (*18 sts*)

Small spot only:

Ss in next st and fasten off.

Large spot only:

Round 4: *1sc in each of next 2 sts, 2sc in next st; rep from * to end. (*24 sts*)

Ss in next st, fasten off.

Press all spots with a damp cloth on WS.

Sew spots onto Hat on front and back of Hat using the photo as a guide.

Honey the bee

The wobbly antennae are what makes this hat so cute. Perfect for buzzing around the park!

Materials

Debbie Bliss Cashmerino Aran, 55% merino wool, 33% acrylic, 12% cashmere worsted (aran) yarn, 1¾oz (50g) balls, approx 98yd (90m) per ball:
- 1 x ball of shade 300 Black (A)
- 1 x ball of shade 077 Gold (yellow) (B)

US size H/8 (5mm) and US size E/4 (3.5mm) crochet hooks

Yarn sewing needle

Gauge

15 sts x 11 rows over a 4in (10cm) square using US size H/8 (5mm) hook, half double crochet, and Cashmerino Aran.

Size

To fit age 6–24 months

Finished measurements

Approx 16–18in (40.5–46cm) circumference, 6½in (16.5cm) high

Abbreviations

approx approximately
beg beginning
ch chain
hdc half double crochet
rep repeat
RS right side
sc single crochet
sc2tog single crochet 2 stitches together
ss slip stitch
st(s) stitch(es)
WS wrong side

Hat

Work in rounds, placing st marker at beg of each round and changing color every two rows.

Round 1: Using A and US size H/8 (5mm) hook, 2ch, 8hdc in second ch from hook. (*8 sts*)
Round 2: 2hdc in each st. Cut yarn, do not fasten off. (*16 sts*)
Round 3: Join B, *1hdc in next st, 2hdc in next st; rep from * to end. (*24 sts*)
Round 4: *1hdc in each of next 2 sts, 2hdc in next st; rep from * to end. (*32 sts*)
Cut yarn, do not fasten off.
Round 5: Using A, *1hdc in each of next 3 sts, 2hdc in next st; rep from * to end. (*40 sts*)
Round 6: *1hdc in each of next 4 sts, 2hdc in next st; rep from * to end. (*48 sts*)
Round 7: Using B, *1hdc in each of next 5 sts, 2hdc in next st; rep from * to end. (*56 sts*)
Round 8: *1hdc in each of next 6 sts, 2hdc in next st; rep from * to end. (*64 sts*)
Continue with this two-row color sequence in following rounds.

Rounds 9–18: 1hdc in each st to end. (*64 sts*)
Next round: 1sc in each st to end, ss in last st.
Fasten off.

Antenna

(make two)
Work on RS throughout.
Round 1: Using A and US size E/4 (3.5mm) hook, 2ch, 6sc in second ch from hook. (*6 sts*)
Round 2: 2sc in each st. (*12 sts*)
Round 3: 1sc in each st to end. (*12 sts*)
Round 4: *1sc in next st, sc2tog; rep from * to end. (*8 sts*)
Sew in end on WS and continue to work on RS.
Round 5: *1sc in each of next 2 sts, sc2tog; rep from * to end. (*6 sts*)
Rounds 6–9: 1sc in each st to end. (*6 sts*)
Ss in next st, fasten off.

Sew on each Antenna approx 4in (10cm) apart, starting 5 rounds from top of Hat.

Tip

This hat is made in two-row
stripes, joining in the new color
in the top of the last
stitch of each round.

cool hats for kids

Archie the owl

A baby owl, made using rows rather than rounds. A great pattern for a beginner who hasn't mastered rounds yet.

Materials

Debbie Bliss Cashmerino Aran, 55% merino wool, 33% acrylic, 12% cashmere worsted (aran) yarn, 1¾oz (50g) balls, approx 98yd (90m) per ball:
  2 x balls of shade 009 Grey (MC)

Debbie Bliss Lara, 58% merino wool, 42% superfine alpaca bulky (super chunky) yarn, 100g (3½oz) balls, approx 65yd (60m) per ball:
  1 x ball of shade 001 Pasha (off white) (A)

Debbie Bliss Baby Cashmerino, 55% wool, 33% acrylic, 12% cashmere sportweight (4ply) yarn, 1¾oz (50g) balls, approx 137yd (125m) per ball:
  1 x ball of shade 100 White (B)
  1 x ball of shade 092 Orange (C)

US size H/8 (5mm) and US size E/4 (3.5mm) crochet hooks

Orange safety eyes or black yarn for embroidered eyes

Off-white thread and sewing needle

Yarn sewing needle

Gauge

16 sts x 16 rows over a 4in (10cm) square using US size H/8 (5mm) hook, single crochet, and Cashmerino Aran.

Size

To fit age 3–10 years

Finished measurements

Approx 18–20in (46–51cm) circumference, 7in (18cm) high

Abbreviations

approx approximately
beg begin(ning)
ch chain
rep repeat
RS right side
sc single crochet
st(s) stitch(es)
WS wrong side

Hat

(Make 2, front and back)
Work in rows, turning at end of each row.
Row 1: Using MC and US size H/8 (5mm) hook, make 37ch, 1sc in second ch from hook, 1sc in each ch to end. Turn. *(36 sts)*
Row 2: 1ch, 1sc in each st to end. *(36 sts)*
Rep Row 2 until work measures approx 33 rows or 7in (18cm). Fasten off.

Press both pieces.
With RS facing, sew sides and top seams of Front and Back together. Turn RS out.

Ears

Make two tassels using A and place one in each corner. Tassel yarn is thicker than yarn used in Hat, so ease loops through as follows: Wrap A around fingers approx 6 times, remove from fingers and insert hook into corner. Pull each of 6 loops through individually by approx ½in (1.25cm) only. When all loops are through, insert hook back through all 6 loops and pull with your fingers to create one hole, with all 6 loops, big enough to pull tails through. Pull all tails through together by inserting your thumb and index finger through hole and pulling tails all through together. Once all tails are through, pull them firmly to secure in place. Cut through end loops of tail and trim to create tassel ears. Using a hairbrush, hold knots of Ears and brush strands of yarn to fluff up.

Eyes

(make two)

Work in rounds, placing st marker at beg of each round.

Round 1: Using B and US size E/4 (3.5mm) hook, make 2ch, 6sc in second ch from hook. *(6 sts)*

Round 2: 2sc in each st to end. *(12 sts)*

Round 3: *1sc in next st, 2sc in next st; rep from * to end. *(18 sts)*

Round 4: *1sc in each of next 2 sts, 2sc in next st; rep from * to end. *(24 sts)*

Round 5: *1sc in each of next 3 sts, 2sc in next st; rep from * to end. *(30 sts)*

Fasten off, leaving long tail for sewing onto Hat.

With RS facing upwards, sew eyes on front of Hat, approx 8 to 9 rows from bottom edge and approx 1 to 2 sts apart. Insert safety eyes in center of crocheted eyes, if using. For embroidered eyes, work a circle in satin stitch (see page 18) in the center of each eye, using C, then a smaller circle using a scrap of black yarn.

Beak

Work in rows, turning at end of each row.

Row 1: Using C and US size E/4 (3.5mm) hook, make 2ch, 3sc in second ch from hook. Turn. *(3 sts)*

Row 2: 1ch, 1sc in each st. *(3 sts)*

Row 3: 1ch, 2sc in first st, 1sc in next st, 2sc in last st. *(5 sts)*

Row 4: 1ch, 2sc in first st, 1sc in each of next 3 sts, 2sc in last st. *(7 sts)*

Fasten off, leaving long yarn tail for sewing to Hat.

Sew Beak to Hat, centered between eyes, with tip of triangle facing downwards and approx 5 rows from bottom edging.

Eyebrows

Cut a piece of yarn B approx 12in (30cm) long. Brush yarn with a hairbrush to fluff it up and loosen fibers. Place yarn in one continuous length around eyes in a curve, with center of curve between both eyes. Pin in place carefully without losing shaping. With a needle and thread, sew yarn strand in place with a few loose running stitches.

Polar bears are normally fierce, but not this one! This bear is so cute and is made in a soft wool/silk mix.

Jolyon the polar bear

Materials

Fyberspates Scrumptious Aran, 55% merino wool, 45% silk worsted (aran) yarn, 100g (3½oz) hanks, approx 180yd (165m) per hank:
   1 x hank of shade 400 Natural (off white) (MC)

Debbie Bliss Rialto Chunky, 100% merino wool bulky (chunky) yarn, 1¾oz (50g) balls, approx 66yd (60m) per ball:
   Small amount of shade 001 Black (A)

US size H/8 (5mm) crochet hook

Small amount of polyester toy stuffing

Yarn sewing needle

Gauge

16 sts x 16 rows over a 4in (10cm) square using US size H/8 (5mm) hook, single crochet, and Scrumptious Aran.

Size

To fit age 3–10 years

Finished measurements

Approx 18–20in (46–51cm) circumference, 7in (18cm) high

Abbreviations

approx approximately
beg begin(ning)
ch chain
dc double crochet
rep repeat
RS right side
sc single crochet
sc2tog single crochet 2 stitches together
ss slip stitch
st(s) stitch(es)
WS wrong side

Hat

Work in rounds, placing st marker at beg of each round.
Round 1: Using MC, 2ch, 6sc in second ch from hook. (*6 sts*)
Round 2: 2sc in each st to end. (*12 sts*)
Round 3: *1sc in next st, 2sc in next st; rep from * to end. (*18 sts*)
Round 4: 1sc in each of next 2 sts, 2sc in next st; rep from * to end. (*24 sts*)
Round 5: *1sc in each of next 3 sts, 2sc in next st; rep from * to end. (*30 sts*)
Round 6: *1sc in each of next 4 sts, 2sc in next st; rep from * to end. (*36 sts*)
Round 7: *1sc in each of next 5 sts, 2sc in next st; rep from * to end. (*42 sts*)
Round 8: *1sc in each of next 6 sts, 2sc in next st; rep from * to end. (*48 sts*)
Round 9: *1sc in each of next 7 sts, 2sc in next st; rep from * to end. (*54 sts*)
Round 10: *1sc in each of next 8 sts, 2sc in next st; rep from * to end. (*60 sts*)
Round 11: *1sc in each of next 9 sts, 2sc in next st; rep from * to end. (*66 sts*)
Rounds 12–28: 1sc in each st to end. (*66 sts*)
Do not fasten off.
Place first st marker here to denote back of hat.

First earflap:

1sc in each of next 6 sts. Do not turn.
Beg working in rows, turning at end of each following row.
Row 1 (RS): 1sc in each of next 15 sts. Turn. (*15 sts*)
Row 2 (WS): 1ch, sc2tog,1sc in each of next 11 sts, sc2tog. (*13 sts*)
Row 3: 1ch, 1sc in each st to end. (*13 sts*)
Row 4: 1ch, sc2tog, 1sc in each of next 9 sts, sc2tog. (*11 sts*)
Row 5: 1ch, 1sc in each st to end. (*11 sts*)
Row 6: 1ch, sc2tog, 1sc in each of next 7 sts, sc2tog. (*9 sts*)
Row 7: 1ch, 1sc in each st to end. (*9 sts*)
Row 8: 1ch, sc2tog, 1sc in each of next 5 sts, sc2tog. (*7 sts*)
Row 9: 1ch, 1sc in each st to end. (*7 sts*)
Row 10: 1ch, sc2tog, 1sc in each of next 3 sts, sc2tog. (*5 sts*)
Rows 11–16: 1ch, 1sc in each st to end. (*5 sts*)
Do not fasten off.

Back paw:

Row 17: 1ch, 2sc in first st, 1sc in each of next 3 sts, 2sc in last st. (*7 sts*)
Row 18: 1ch, 2sc in first st, 1sc in each of next 5 sts, 2sc in last st. (*9 sts*)
Rows 19–21: 1ch, 1sc in each st to end. (*9 sts*)
Row 22: 1ch, sc2tog, 1sc in each of next 5 sts, sc2tog. (*7 sts*)
Row 23: 1ch, sc2tog, 1sc in each of next 3 sts, sc2tog. (*5 sts*)
Row 24: 1ch, sc2tog, 1sc in next st, sc2tog. (*3 sts*)

Front paw:
Row 25: 1ch, 1sc in each st to end. (*3 sts*)
Row 26: 1ch, 2sc in first st, 1sc in next st, 2sc in next st. (*5 sts*)
Row 27: 1ch, 2sc in first st, 1sc in each of next 3 sts, 2sc in next st. (*7 sts*)
Row 28: 1ch, 2sc in first st, 1sc in each of next 5 sts, 2sc in next st. (*9 sts*)
Rows 29–31: 1ch, 1sc in each st to end. (*9 sts*)
Row 32: 1ch, sc2tog, 1sc in each of next 5 sts, sc2tog. (*7 sts*)
Row 34: 1ch, sc2tog, 1sc in each of next 3 sts, sc2tog. (*5 sts*)
Row 35: 1ch, 1sc in each st to end. (*5 sts*)
Fasten off leaving a long tail for sewing up Paw.

Second earflap:
With RS facing, join MC in next st along from end of Row 1 of First earflap.
1ch, 1sc in same st, 1sc in each of next 11 sts, place second st marker here to denote front of hat, 1sc in each of next 12 sts. Do not turn. (*24 sts*)
Work in rows, turning at end of each row.
Row 1 (RS): 1sc in each of next 15 sts. Turn.
Rep Rows 2–35 of First earflap to end of Paws.

Fold bottom Paw to wrong side of top Paw and sew all round using long tail.
Using A, embroider two Claws in straight stitch (see page 18) on each Paw, using the photo as a guide.

Muzzle

Work in rounds, placing st marker at beg of each round.

Round 1: Using MC, make 2ch, 6sc in second ch from hook. *(6 sts)*

Round 2: 2sc in each st to end. *(12 sts)*

Round 3: *1sc in next st, 2sc in next st; rep from * to end. *(18 sts)*

Round 4: *1sc in each of next 2 sts, 2sc in next st; rep from * to end. *(24 sts)*

Round 5: 1sc in each st to end. *(24 sts)*

Ss in next st.

Fasten off leaving a long tail for sewing on.

Center Muzzle approx 1 row up from bottom edge. Stitch in place leaving small gap before stuffing lightly. Continue to close gap and sew in end.

Mouth and eyes

Using A, embroider nose in satin stitch (see page 18) and mouth in backstitch. Using A, embroider eyes in satin stitch approx 13 rows from bottom edge and 8 sts apart.

Ears

(make 2)

Work in rounds, placing st marker at beg of each round.

Round 1: Using MC, make 2ch, 6sc in second ch from hook.

Round 2: 2sc in each st to end. *(12 sts)*

Round 3: *1sc in each of next 2 sts, 2sc in next st; rep from * to end. *(16 sts)*

Round 4: *1sc in each of next 3 sts, 2sc in next st; rep from * to end. *(20 sts)*

Rounds 5–9: 1sc in each st to end.

Ss in next st.

Fasten off, leaving a long tail for sewing on.

Sew in end from starting point.

With straight edges of ears flat and using long tail, sew onto Hat approx 3in (7.5cm) apart, and starting approx 6 rounds down from top.

A great companion to the Cockerel (see page 102). If you'd like to make this for an adult use the pattern for the hat from the Cockerel, and make the details (eyes, comb, beak) using this pattern.

Limoney the chicken

Materials
Debbie Bliss Cashmerino Aran, 55% merino wool, 33% acrylic, 12% cashmere worsted (aran) yarn, 1¾oz (50g) balls, approx 98yd (90m) per ball:
   1 x ball of shade 101 Ecru (off white) (MC)

Debbie Bliss Rialto DK, 100% merino wool light worsted (DK) yarn, 1¾oz (50g) balls, approx 115yd (105m) per ball:
   1 x ball of shade 12 Scarlet (A)

Fyberspates Vivacious DK, 100% merino wool light worsted (DK) yarn, 115g (4oz) hank, approx 253yd (230m) per hank:
   Scrap of shade 804 Sunshine (B)

Scrap of black yarn

US size H/8 (5mm) and US size G/4 (4mm) crochet hooks

Yarn sewing needle

Gauge
15 sts x 11 rows over a 4in (10cm) square using US size H/8 (5mm) hook, half double crochet, and Cashmerino Aran.

Size
To fit age 3–10 years

Finished measurements
Approx 18–20in (46–51cm) circumference, 7in (18cm) high

Abbreviations
approx approximately
beg begin(ning)
ch chain
sc single crochet
hdc half double crochet
rep repeat
RS right side
ss slip stitch
st(s) stitch(es)
tr treble
dc double crochet
dc3tog double crochet 3 stitches together
WS wrong side

Hat
Work in rounds, placing st marker at beg of each round.
Round 1: Using MC and US size H/8 (5mm) hook, make 2ch, 4hdc in second ch from hook. (4 sts)
Round 2: 2hdc in each st to end. (8 sts)
Round 3: Rep Round 2. (16 sts)
Round 4: *1hdc in next st, 2hdc in next st; rep from * to end. (24 sts)
Round 5: *1hdc in each of next 2 sts, 2hdc in next st; rep from * to end. (32 sts)
Round 6: *1hdc in each of next 3 sts, 2hdc in next st; rep from * to end. (40 sts)
Round 7: *1hdc in each of next 4 sts, 2hdc in next st; rep from * to end. (48 sts)
Round 8: *1hdc in each of next 5 sts, 2hdc in next st; rep from * to end. (56 sts)

Round 9: *1hdc in each of next 6 sts, 2hdc in next st; rep from * to end. (64 sts)
Rounds 10–21: 1hdc in each st to end. (64 sts)
Round 22: 1sc in each st to end.
Do not fasten off.
Place first st marker here to denote back of hat.

First earflap:
1sc in each of next 6 sts. Do not turn.
Beg working in rows, turning at end of each row.
Row 1 (RS): 1sc in each of next 15 sts. Turn. (15 sts)
Row 2 (WS): 1ch, sc2tog, 1sc in each of next 11 sts, sc2tog. (13 sts)
Row 3: 1ch, 1sc in each st to end. (13 sts)
Row 4: 1ch, sc2tog, 1sc in each of next 9 sts, sc2tog. (11 sts)
Row 5: 1ch, 1sc in each st to end. (11 sts)
Row 6: 1ch, sc2tog, 1sc in each of next 7 sts, sc2tog. (9 sts)

Row 1: 1sc in each of next 15 sts. Turn.
Rep Rows 2–14 of First earflap.
Note: front of hat is widest straight edge.

Edging:
With RS of work facing, rejoin MC at back of work at start of straight edging after Earflap.
1ch, 1sc in same st, 1sc in each of next 13 sts along back of Hat to start of Earflap, make 11 sc evenly down first edge of first Earflap, **2sc in first of 3 sts at bottom edge, 1sc in next st, 2sc in next st, make 11 sc evenly along other edge of Earflap**, 1sc in each of next 21 sts along front of Hat, make 11 sc evenly along first edge of next Earflap; rep from ** to **, join with a ss in first sc. *(89 sts)*
Fasten off.

Foot
(make 2)
On RS of hat join A in center st of 3 sts on edge of one Earflap, make 35ch.
Claw 1: Ss in second ch from hook, ss in each of next 4 sts. *(5 sts)*
Claw 2: 6ch, ss in second ch from hook, ss in each of next 4 sts. *(5 sts)*
Claw 3: 6ch, ss in second ch from hook, ss in each of next 4 sts. *(5 sts)*
Ss in base of Claw 1 to form foot.
Ss in each of next 29 ch along leg back to Earflap, join with a ss in same place as joining stitch.
Fasten off.
Rep on other Earflap to make Foot 2.

Comb
Work in rows, turning at end of each row.
Row 1: Using A and US size G/4 (4mm) hook, make 20ch leaving a long tail at beginning, 1sc in second ch from hook, 1sc in each ch to end. Turn. *(19 sts)*
Row 2: 1ch, 1sc in first st, *skip 2 sts, 5dc in next st, skip 2 sts, 1sc in next st; rep from * to end.
Row 3: 1ch, 1sc in first st, *1hdc in next st, 2dc in next st, 5tr in next st, 2dc in next st, 1hdc in next st, 1sc in next st; rep from * to end.
Fasten off.
Center Comb on top of hat, running from front of Hat to back (not side to side). Pin and sew on using long tail.

Beak
(make 2)
Work in rows, turning at end of each row.
Row 1: Using B and US size G/4 (4mm) hook, make 2ch, 3sc in second ch from hook. Turn. *(3 sts)*
Row 2: 1ch, 2sc in first st, 1sc in next st, 2sc in last st. *(5 sts)*
Row 3: 1ch, 1sc in each st to end. *(5 sts)*
Row 4: 1ch, 2sc in first st, 1sc in each of next 3 sts, 2sc in last st. *(7 sts)*
Row 5: 1ch, 1sc in each st to end. *(7 sts)*
Row 6: 1ch, 2sc in first st, 1sc in each of next 5 sts, 2sc in last st. *(9 sts)*

Row 7: 1ch, 1sc in each st to end. *(9 sts)*
Row 8: 1ch, sc2tog, 1sc in each of next 5 sts, sc2tog. *(7 sts)*
Row 9: 1ch, 1sc in each st to end. *(7 sts)*
Row 10: 1ch, sc2tog, 1sc in each of next 3 sts. *(5 sts)*
Row 11: 1ch, 1sc in each st to end. *(5 sts)*
Row 12: 1ch, sc2tog, 1sc in next st, sc2tog. *(3 sts)*
Rows 13–14: 1ch, 1sc in each st to end. *(3 sts)*
Fasten off.

Second earflap:
With RS facing, join MC in next st along from end of Row 1 of First earflap.
1ch, 1sc in same st, 1sc in each of next 10 sts, place second st marker here to denote front of hat, 1sc in each of next 11 sts. Do not turn. *(22 sts)*
Work in rows, turning at end of each row.

Row 7: 1ch, 1sc in each st to end. (9 sts)

Row 8: 1ch, sc2tog, 1sc in each of next 5 sts, sc2tog. (7 sts)

Row 9: 1ch, 1sc in each st to end. (7 sts)

Row 10: 1ch, sc2tog, 1sc in each of next 3 sts, sc2tog. (5 sts)

Row 11: 1ch, 1sc in each st to end. (5 sts)

Row 12: 1ch, sc2tog, 1sc in next st, sc2tog. (3 sts)

Row 13: Dc3tog (diamond made). Do not fasten off.

Row 14: 1ch, 3sc in top of dc3tog.

Row 15: 1ch, 2sc in first st, 1sc in next st, 2sc in last st. (5 sts)

Row 16: 1ch, 1sc in each st to end. (5 sts)

Row 17: 1ch, 2sc in first st, 1sc in each of next 3 sts, 2sc in last st. (7 sts)

Row 18: 1ch, 1sc in each st to end. (7 sts)

Row 19: 1ch, 2sc in first st, 1sc in each of next 5 sts, 2sc in last st. (9 sts)

Fasten off leaving a long tail for sewing up.

With WS together, fold up triangle just made to halfway up diamond. Sew two sides of triangle, turn right side out. Then sew last edge of triangle.

Center at bottom edge, with double triangle overlapping single triangle, and sew beak to Hat.

Eyes

Using scrap of black yarn, embroider eyes in satin stitch (see page 18) approx 6 sts apart.

Not-so-growly Grizzly. This bear hat is made using single crochet and has lovely warm earflaps. A very lovely hat to make—but you'll need good lighting as the wool is dark and the stitches more difficult to see in soft light.

Curtis the grizzly bear

Materials
Debbie Bliss Falkland Aran, 100% wool aran (worsted) yarn, 100g (1¾oz) hanks, approx 109yd (108m) per hank:
> 1 x hank of shade 04 Chocolate (brown) (MC)
> Scrap of shade 16 Blossom (pink) (B)

Debbie Bliss Rialto DK, 100% merino wool light worsted (DK) yarn, 1¾oz (50g) balls, approx 115yd (105m) per ball:
> Scrap of shade 03 Black (A)
> Scrap of Shade 01 White (C)

US size H/8 (5mm) crochet hook

Small amount of polyester toy stuffing (or brown ends of yarn)

Yarn sewing needle

Gauge
16 sts x 16 rows over a 4in (10cm) square using US size H/8 (5mm) hook, single crochet, and Falkland Aran.

Size
To fit age 3–10 years

Finished measurements
Approx 18–20in (46–51cm) circumference, 7in (18cm) high

Abbreviations
approx approximately
beg begin(ning)
ch chain
dc double crochet
rep repeat
RS right side
sc single crochet
sc2tog single crochet 2 stitches together
ss slip stitch
st(s) stitch(es)
WS wrong side

Hat
Work in rounds, placing st marker at beg of each round.
Round 1: Using MC, 2ch, 6sc in second ch from hook. (*6 sts*)
Round 2: 2sc in each st to end. (*12 sts*)
Round 3: *1sc in next st, 2sc in next st; rep from * to end. (*18 sts*)
Round 4: *1sc in each of next 2 sts, 2sc in next st; rep from * to end. (*24 sts*)
Round 5: *1sc in each of next 3 sts, 2sc in next st; rep from * to end. (*30 sts*)
Round 6: *1sc in each of next 4 sts, 2sc in next st; rep from * to end. (*36 sts*)
Round 7: *1sc in each of next 5 sts, 2sc in next st; rep from * to end. (*42 sts*)
Round 8: *1sc in each of next 6 sts, 2sc in next st; rep from * to end. (*48 sts*)
Round 9: *1sc in each of next 7 sts, 2sc in next st; rep from * to end. (*54 sts*)
Round 10: *1sc in each of next 8 sts, 2sc in next st; rep from * to end. (*60 sts*)
Round 11: *1sc in each of next 9 sts, 2sc in next st; rep from * to end. (*66 sts*)
Rounds 12–28: 1sc in each st to end. (*66 sts*)
Do not fasten off.
Place first st marker here to denote back of Hat.

First earflap:

1sc in each of next 6 sts. Do not turn.

Beg working in rows, turning at end of each following row.

Row 1 (RS): 1sc in each of next 15 sts. Turn. *(15 sts)*

Row 2 (WS): 1ch, sc2tog, 1sc in each of next 11 sts, sc2tog. *(13 sts)*

Row 3: 1ch, 1sc in each st to end. *(13 sts)*

Row 4: 1ch, sc2tog, 1sc in each of next 9 sts, sc2tog. *(11 sts)*

Row 5: 1ch, 1sc in each st to end. *(11 sts)*

Row 6: 1ch, sc2tog, 1sc in each of next 7 sts, sc2tog. *(9 sts)*

Row 7: 1ch, 1sc in each st to end. *(9 sts)*

Row 8: 1ch, sc2tog, 1sc in each of next 5 sts, sc2tog. *(7 sts)*

Row 9: 1ch, 1sc in each st to end. *(7 sts)*

Row 10: 1ch, sc2tog, 1sc in each of next 3 sts, sc2tog. *(5 sts)*

Row 11: 1ch, 1sc in each st to end. *(5 sts)*

Row 12: 1ch, sc2tog, 1sc in next st, sc2tog. *(3 sts)*

Rows 13–14: 1ch, 1sc in each st to end. *(3 sts)*

Fasten off.

Second earflap:

With RS facing, join MC in next st along from end of Row 1 of First earflap.

1ch, 1sc in same st, 1sc in each of next 11 sts, place second st marker here to denote front of Hat, 1sc in each of next 12 sts. Do not turn. *(24 sts)*

Work in rows, turning at end of each following row.

Row 1: 1sc in each of next 15 sts. Turn.

Rep Rows 2–14 of First earflap.

Edging:

With RS of work facing, rejoin MC at back of work at start of straight edging after second Earflap.

1ch, 1sc in same st, 1sc in each of next 11 sts along back of Hat to start of Earflap, make 12 sc evenly down first edge of first Earflap, **2sc in first of 3 sts at bottom edge, 1sc in next st, 2sc in next st, make 12 sc evenly along other edge of Earflap**, 1sc in each of next 24 sts along front of Hat, make 12 sc evenly along first edge of next Earflap; rep from ** to **, join with a ss in first sc. *(94 sts)*

Fasten off.

Muzzle

Work in rounds, placing st marker at beg of each round.

Round 1: Using MC, make 2ch, 6sc in second ch from hook. *(6 sts)*

Round 2: 2sc in each st to end. *(12 sts)*

Round 3: *1sc in next st, 2sc in next st; rep from * to end. *(18 sts)*

Round 4: *1sc in each of next 2 sts, 2sc in next st; rep from * to end. *(24 sts)*

Round 5: *1sc in each of next 3 sts, 2sc in next st; rep from * to end. *(30 sts)*

Ss in next st.

Fasten off.

Nose

Work in rounds, placing st marker at beg of each round.

Round 1: Using A, make 2ch, 6sc in second ch from hook. *(6 sts)*

Round 2: 2sc in each st to end. *(12 sts)*

Round 3: *1sc in next st, 2sc in next st; rep from * to end. *(18 sts)*

Rounds 4–5: 1sc in each st to end. *(18 sts)*

Round 6: *1sc in next st, sc2tog; rep from * to end. *(12 sts)*

Round 7: 1sc in each st to end. *(12 sts)*

Fasten off, leaving a long tail.

Weave length of yarn left after fastening off through last round of sts. Pull yarn tightly to gather and sew to secure. Leave length of yarn to sew onto Muzzle.

Sew Muzzle to front of Hat with muzzle edge at bottom edge of hat, leaving a small gap and stuff muzzle with toy stuffing or brown scraps of yarn.

Sew Nose onto Muzzle.

Ears

(make 2)

Work in rounds, placing st marker at beg of each round.

Using MC, make 4ch, join with a ss to form a ring.

Round 1: 1ch, 12sc in ring, join with a ss in first sc. *(12 sts)*

Round 2: 1ch, 2sc in each st to end, join with a ss in first sc. *(24 sts)*

Rounds 3–4: 1ch, 1sc in each st to end. *(24 sts)*

Fasten off leaving a long tail for sewing on later.

Sew around hole in center and pull to close.

Sew Ears in place at top of Hat at center, approx 3½in (9cm) apart and starting approx 5 rounds down from top.

Mouth and eyes

Using B, embroider the mouth in straight stitch (see page 18) onto Muzzle under Nose.

Using A and C, embroider eyes in satin stitch (see page 18) approx one row above Muzzle and 10 sts apart.

Donny the donkey

One of the cutest animals—I love their big furry ears, fuzzy mane, and long face.

Materials

Debbie Bliss Falkland Aran, 100% wool worsted (aran) yarn, 100g (3½oz) hanks, approx 196yd (180m) per hank:

    1 x hank of shade 04 Chocolate (brown) (MC)

    1 x hank of shade 05 Camel (beige) (A)

Small amount of black bulky (chunky) yarn (B)

US size H/8 (5mm) and US size E/4 (3.5mm) crochet hooks

15mm brown and black safety eyes

Small amount of polyester toy stuffing

Yarn sewing needle

Gauge

16 sts x 16 rows over a 4in (10cm) square using US size H/8 (5mm) hook, single crochet, and Falkland Aran.

Size

To fit age 3–10 years

Finished measurements

Approx 18–20in (46–51cm) circumference, 7in (18cm) high

Abbreviations

approx approximately
beg beginning
ch chain
rep repeat
RS right side
sc single crochet
sc2tog single crochet 2 stitches together
ss slip stitch
st(s) stitch(es)
WS wrong side

Hat

Work in rounds, placing st marker at beg of each round.

Round 1: Using MC and US size H/8 (5mm) hook, 2ch, 6sc in second ch from hook. *(6 sts)*

Round 2: 2sc in each st to end. *(12 sts)*

Round 3: *1sc in next st, 2sc in next st; rep from * to end. *(18 sts)*

Round 4: *1sc in each of next 2 sts, 2sc in next st; rep from * to end. *(24 sts)*

Round 5: *1sc in each of next 3 sts, 2sc in next st; rep from * to end. *(30 sts)*

Round 6: *1sc in each of next 4 sts, 2sc in next st; rep from * to end. *(36 sts)*

Round 7: *1sc in each of next 5 sts, 2sc in next st; rep from * to end. *(42 sts)*

Round 8: *1sc in each of next 6 sts, 2sc in next st; rep from * to end. *(48 sts)*

Round 9: *1sc in each of next 7 sts, 2sc in next st; rep from * to end. *(54 sts)*

Round 10: *1sc in each of next 8 sts, 2sc in next st; rep from * to end. *(60 sts)*

Round 11: *1sc in each of next 9 sts, 2sc in next st; rep from * to end. *(66 sts)*

Rounds 12–28: 1sc in each st to end. *(66 sts)*

Do not fasten off.

Place first st marker here to denote center back of Hat.

Second earflap:
With RS facing, join MC in next st along from end of Row 1 of First earflap.
1ch, 1sc in same st, 1sc in each of next 11 sts, place second st marker here to denote center front of Hat, 1sc in each of next 12 sts. Do not turn. *(24 sts)*
Work in rows, turning at end of each row.
Row 1 (RS): 1sc in each of next 15 sts. Turn.
Rep Rows 2–12 of First earflap.

Muzzle
Work in rounds, placing st marker at beg of each round.
Round 1: Using A and US size E/4 (3.5mm) hook, make 2ch, 6sc in second ch from hook. *(6 sts)*
Round 2: 2sc in each st to end. *(12 sts)*
Round 3: *1sc in next st, 2sc in next st; rep from * to end. *(18 sts)*
Round 4: *1sc in each of next 2 sts, 2sc in next st; rep from * to end. *(24 sts)*
Round 5: *1sc in each of next 3 sts, 2sc in next st; rep from * to end. *(30 sts)*
Round 6: *1sc in each of next 4 sts, 2sc in next st; rep from * to end. *(36 sts)*
Rounds 7–11: 1sc in each st to end. *(36 sts)*
Ss in next st.
Fasten off leaving long tail for sewing on.

Center Muzzle at front of Hat approx 1 row up from bottom edge. Leave small gap before stuffing lightly. Continue to close gap and sew in end.

Using B, embroider nostrils using French knots (see page 19).

Outer ear
(make 2)
Work in rows, turning at end of each row.
Row 1: Using MC and US size H/8 (5mm) hook, make 2ch, 3sc in second ch from hook. Turn. *(3 sts)*
Row 2: 1ch (does not count as st), 2sc in first st, 1sc in next st, 2sc in last st. *(5 sts)*
Row 3: 1ch, 1sc in each st to end. *(5 sts)*
Row 4: 1ch, 2sc in first st, 1sc in each of next 3 sts, 2sc in last st. *(7 sts)*
Row 5: 1ch, 1sc in each st to end. *(7 sts)*
Row 6: 1ch, 2sc in first st, 1sc in each of next 5 sts, 2sc in last st. *(9 sts)*
Row 7: 1ch, 1sc in each st to end. *(9 sts)*

First earflap:
1sc in each of next 6 sts. Do not turn.
Beg working in rows, turning at end of each following row.
Row 1 (RS): 1sc in each of next 15 sts. Turn. *(15 sts)*
Row 2 (WS): 1ch (does not count as st throughout), sc2tog,1sc in each of next 11 sts, sc2tog. *(13 sts)*
Row 3: 1ch, 1sc in each st to end. *(13 sts)*
Row 4: 1ch, sc2tog, 1sc in each of next 9 sts, sc2tog. *(11 sts)*
Row 5: 1ch, 1sc in each st to end. *(11 sts)*
Row 6: 1ch, sc2tog, 1sc in each of next 7 sts, sc2tog. *(9 sts)*
Row 7: 1ch, 1sc in each st to end. *(9 sts)*
Row 8: 1ch, sc2tog, 1sc in each of next 5 sts, sc2tog. *(7 sts)*
Row 9: 1ch, 1sc in each st to end. *(7 sts)*
Row 10: 1ch, sc2tog, 1sc in each of next 3 sts, sc2tog. *(5 sts)*
Row 11: 1ch, sc2tog, 1sc in next st, sc2tog. *(3 sts)*
Row 12: 1ch, 1sc in each st.
Fasten off.

Row 8: 1ch, 2sc in first st, 1sc in each of next 7 sts, 2sc in last st. *(11 sts)*

Row 9: 1ch, 1sc in each st to end. *(11 sts)*

Row 10: 1ch, 2sc in first st, 1sc in each of next 9 sts, 2sc in last st. *(13 sts)*

Rows 11–25: 1ch, 1sc in each st to end. *(13 sts)*
Fasten off, leaving long tail for sewing inner ear to outer ear.

Inner ear
(make 2)
Work in rows, turning at end of each row.

Row 1: Using A and US size E/4 (3.5mm) hook, make 2ch, 3sc in second ch from hook. Turn. *(3 sts)*

Row 2: 1ch, 2sc in first st, 1sc in next st, 2sc in last st. *(5 sts)*

Rows 3–4: 1ch, 1sc in each st to end. *(5 sts)*

Row 5: 1ch, 2sc in first st, 1sc in each of next 3 sts, 2sc in last st. *(7 sts)*

Rows 6–7: 1ch, 1sc in each st to end. *(7 sts)*

Row 8: 1ch, 2sc in first st, 1sc in each of next 5 sts, 2sc in last st. *(9 sts)*

Rows 9–25: 1ch, 1sc in each st to end. *(9 sts)*
Fasten off.

With RS together, pin and sew outside edges of Inner ear and Outer ear together leaving bottom edge open. Turn RS out.
Position Ears on top of Hat, approx 3½in (9cm) apart at top. Shape outer edges of ears towards middle, and pin and sew in place.

Eyes
(make 2)
Work in rounds, placing st marker at beg of each round.
Using A and US size E/4 (3.5mm) hook, and leaving a long end of approx 6in (15cm), make 2ch, make 6sc into second ch from hook, join with ss to form a ring.

Round 1: 1ch, 1sc in next st, 2sc in each of next 5 sts, join with a ss in first sc. *(11 sts)*

Round 2: 1ch, 1sc in each st to end, join with a ss in first sc. *(11 sts)*

Round 3: 1ch, skip first st, sc2tog around, join with a ss in first sc.
Fasten off leaving a long tail.

Sew in ends but do not cut tails.
Turn eye RS out. Insert safety eyes into center of eye.
Use one yarn tail to stuff center of eye and other yarn tail to sew onto Hat either side of muzzle approx 9 rows from bottom edge and 5in (12.5cm) apart.

Mane
Using B, cut approx 30 lengths each approx 4in (10cm) and make tassel with each strand around Rounds 1 and 2 of Hat at top.

This is a great hat for springtime; a bouncy rabbit with pretty flowers.

Rebecca the flower patch rabbit

Materials

Hat

Debbie Bliss Cashmerino Aran, 55% merino wool, 33% acrylic, 12% cashmere worsted (aran) yarn, 1¾oz (50g) balls, approx 98yd (90m) per ball:
- 1 x ball of shade 27 Stone (pale gray) (MC)
- 1 x ball of shade 101 Ecru (off white) (A)

Flowers

Scraps of each of the following:
- Open Rose: bright pink
- 6-petal flower 1: A: mint green, B: pink
- 6-petal flower 2: A: pale blue, B: turquoise
- Leaves: green
- Blossom 1: A: orange, B: yellow
- Blossom 2: A: pale pink, B: purple

US size H/8 (5mm) and US size E/4 (3.5mm) crochet hooks

Yarn sewing needle

Gauge

15 sts x 11 rows over a 4in (10cm) square using US size H/8 (5mm) hook, half double crochet, and Cashmerino Aran.

Size

To fit age 3–10 years

Finished measurements

Approx 18–20in (46–51cm) circumference, 7in (18cm) high

Abbreviations

approx approximately
beg begin(ning)
ch chain
ch sp chain space
dc double crochet
dtr double treble
hdc half double crochet
rep repeat
RS right side
sc single crochet
ss slip stitch
st(s) stitch(es)
tr treble
WS wrong side

Hat

Work in rounds, placing st marker at beg of each round.

Round 1: Using MC and US size H/8 (5mm) hook, make 2ch, 4hdc in second ch from hook. (*4 sts*)

Round 2: 2hdc in each st to end. (*8 sts*)

Round 3: Rep Round 2. (*16 sts*)

Round 4: *1hdc in next st, 2hdc in next st; rep from * to end. (*24 sts*)

Round 5: *1hdc in each of next 2 sts, 2hdc in next st; rep from * to end. (*32 sts*)

Round 6: *1hdc in each of next 3 sts, 2hdc in next st; rep from * to end. (*40 sts*)

Round 7: *1hdc in each of next 4 sts, 2hdc in next st; rep from * to end. (*48 sts*)

Round 8: *1hdc in each of next 5 sts, 2hdc in next st; rep from * to end. (*56 sts*)

Round 9: *1hdc in each of next 6 sts, 2hdc in next st; rep from * to end. (*64 sts*)

Round 10: *1hdc in each of next 7 sts, 2hdc in next st; rep from * to end. (*72 sts*)

Rounds 11–22: 1hdc in each st to end. (*72 sts*)

Last round: 1sc in each st to end, ss in last st. Do not fasten off.

Outer ear

(*make 2*)

Work in rows, turning at end of each row.

Row 1: Using MC and US size E/4 (3.5mm) hook, make 2ch, 3sc in second ch from hook. Turn. (*3 sts*)

Row 2: 1ch (does not count as st throughout), 2sc in first st, 1sc in next st, 2sc in last st. (*5 sts*)

Row 3: 1ch, 1sc in each st to end. (*5 sts*)

Row 4: 1ch, 2sc in first st, 1sc in each of next 3 sts, 2sc in last st. *(7 sts)*
Row 5: 1ch, 1sc in each st to end. *(7 sts)*
Row 6: 1ch, 2sc in first st, 1sc in each of next 5 sts, 2sc in last st. *(9 sts)*
Row 7: 1ch, 1sc in each st to end. *(9 sts)*
Row 8: 1ch, 2sc in first st, 1sc in each of next 7 sts, 2sc in last st. *(11 sts)*
Row 9: 1ch, 1sc in each st to end. *(11 sts)*
Row 10: 1ch, 2sc in first st, 1sc in each of next 9 sts, 2sc in last st. *(13 sts)*
Rows 11–23: 1ch, 1sc in each st to end. *(13 sts)*
Fasten off, leaving long tail for sewing Inner ear to Outer ear.

Inner ear
(make 2)
Work in rows, turning at end of each row.
Row 1: Using A and US size E/4 (3.5mm) hook, make 2ch, 3sc in second ch from hook. Turn. *(3 sts)*
Row 2: 1ch, 2sc in first st, 1sc in next st, 2sc in last st. *(5 sts)*
Rows 3–4: 1ch, 1sc in each st to end. *(5 sts)*
Row 5: 1ch, 2sc in first st, 1sc in each of next 3 sts, 2sc in last st. *(7 sts)*
Rows 6–7: 1ch, 1sc in each st to end. *(7 sts)*
Row 8: 1ch, 2sc in first st, 1sc in each of next 5 sts, 2sc in last st. *(9 sts)*
Rows 9–23: 1ch, 1sc in each st to end. *(9 sts)*
Fasten off.

With RS together, pin and sew outside edges of Inner ear and Outer ear together leaving bottom edge open. Turn RS out. Lightly stuff Ears and sew up bottom opening.

Position Ears on top of Hat, approx 1in (2.5cm) apart at top. Shape outer edges of ears towards middle, and pin and sew in place.

Open rose
Using bright pink and US size E/4 (3.5mm) hook, 5ch, join with a ss in first ch to form a ring.
Round 1: [1sc, 1dc, 1sc] into ring, 4 times. *(4 petals)*
Round 2: Working with RS facing, [2ch, from WS ss into base of second sc of next petal (pick up 2 loops)] 4 times. *(4 loops)*
Round 3: [4dc into next 2ch sp (loop at just made in Round 2), ss into same ch sp] 4 more times.
Fasten off.

6-petal flower
(make 2, one in each colorway)
Using A and US size E/4 (3.5mm) hook, 4ch, join with a ss in first ch to form a ring.
Round 1 (RS): 1ch, 5sc in ring, cut yarn, do not fasten off, join B with a ss in first sc.
Round 2: *[4ch, 1tr, 4ch, 1ss] in next st; rep from * 5 times more *(6 petals)*, working last ss in sc at base of first 4ch.
Fasten off.
Sew in ends.

Leaves
(make 3)
Using green and US size E/4 (3.5mm) hook, make 8ch, 1sc in second ch from hook, 1hdc in next ch, 1dc in each of next 2 ch, 2sc in next ch, 1hdc in next ch, 1sc in next ch, 2ch. Turn.
Working on underside of first 8ch, 1sc in first ch, 1hdc in next ch, 1dc in each of next 2ch, 2dc in next ch, 1hdc in next ch, 1sc in last ch, join with a ss in tip of leaf.
Fasten off.

Blossoms
(make 2, one in each colorway)
Using A and US size E/4 (3.5mm) hook, make 4ch, join with a ss to form a ring.
Round 1: 2ch, 9sc in ring, cut yarn, do not fasten off. Using B, ss in top of first 2-ch. *(10 sts)*
Round 2: 1ch *[1tr, 2dtr, 1tr] in next sc, ss in next sc; rep from * 3 times more, [1tr, 2dtr, 1tr] in next sc, ss in first 1-ch. *(5 petals)*
Fasten off.

Sew Flowers and Leaves to top front of Hat, using the photo as a guide.

A pretty Palomino for all the pony-lovers who need warm heads!

Phoebe the pony

Materials

Debbie Bliss Cashmerino Aran, 55% merino wool, 33% acrylic, 12% cashmere worsted (aran) yarn, 1¾oz (50g) balls, approx 98yd (90m) per ball:
   1 x ball of shade 066 Mustard (MC)
   1 x ball of shade 101 Ecru (off white) (A)

Small amount of black light worsted (DK) yarn (B)

US size H/8 (5mm) and US size E/4 (3.5mm) crochet hooks

Yarn sewing needle

Gauge

15 sts x 11 rows over a 4in (10cm) square using US size H/8 (5mm) hook, half double crochet, and Cashmerino Aran.

Size

To fit age 3–10 years

Finished measurements

Approx 18–20in (46–51cm) circumference, 7in (18cm) high

Abbreviations

approx approximately
beg begin(ning)
ch chain
hdc half double crochet
rep repeat
RS right side
sc single crochet
sc2tog single crochet 2 stitches together
ss slip stitch
st(s) stitch(es)
WS wrong side

Hat

Work in rounds, placing st marker at beg of each round.

Round 1: Using MC and US size H/8 (5mm) hook, make 2ch, 4hdc in second ch from hook. (*4 sts*)

Round 2: 2hdc in each st to end. (*8 sts*)

Round 3: Rep Round 2. (*16 sts*)

Round 4: *1hdc in next st, 2hdc in next st; rep from * to end. (*24 sts*)

Round 5: *1hdc in each of next 2 sts, 2hdc in next st; rep from * to end. (*32 sts*)

Round 6: *1hdc in each of next 3 sts, 2hdc in next st; rep from * to end. (*40 sts*)

Round 7: *1hdc in each of next 4 sts, 2hdc in next st; rep from * to end. (*48 sts*)

Round 8: *1hdc in each of next 5 sts, 2hdc in next st; rep from * to end. (*56 sts*)

Round 9: *1hdc in each of next 6 sts, 2hdc in next st; rep from * to end. (*64 sts*)

Rounds 10–22: 1hdc in each st to end. (*64 sts*)

Round 23: 1sc in each st to end.

Do not fasten off.

Place first st marker here to denote center back of hat.

First earflap:

1sc in each of next 6 sts. Do not turn.

Beg working in rows, turning at end of each row.

Row 1 (RS): 1sc in each of next 15 sts. Turn. (*15 sts*)

Row 2 (WS): 1ch (does not count as st throughout), sc2tog, 1sc in each of next 11 sts, sc2tog. (*13 sts*)

Row 3: 1ch, 1sc in each st to end. (*13 sts*)

Row 4: 1ch, sc2tog, 1sc in each of next 9 sts, sc2tog. (*11 sts*)

Row 5: 1ch, 1sc in each st to end. (*11 sts*)

Row 6: 1ch, sc2tog, 1sc in each of next 7 sts, sc2tog. (*9 sts*)

Row 7: 1ch, 1sc in each st to end. (*9 sts*)

Row 8: 1ch, sc2tog, 1sc in each of next 5 sts, sc2tog. (*7 sts*)

Row 9: 1ch, 1sc in each st to end. (*7 sts*)

Row 10: 1ch, sc2tog, 1sc in each of next 3 sts, sc2tog. (*5 sts*)

Row 11: 1ch, 1sc in each st to end. (*5 sts*)

Row 12: 1ch, sc2tog, 1sc in next st, sc2tog. (*3 sts*)

Rows 13–14: 1ch, 1sc in each st to end. (*3 sts*)

Fasten off.

Second earflap:
With RS facing, join MC in next st along from end of Row 1 of First earflap.

1ch, 1sc in same st, 1sc in each of next 10 sts, place second st marker here to denote center front of hat, 1sc in each of next 11 sts. Do not turn. (22 sts)

Work in rows, turning at end of each row.

Row 1: 1sc in each of next 15 sts. Turn.

Rep Rows 2–14 of First earflap.

Note: front of hat is widest straight edge.

Edging:
With RS of work facing, rejoin MC at back of work at start of straight edging after Earflap.

1ch, 1sc in same st, 1sc in each of next 13 sts along back of Hat to start of Earflap, make 11 sc evenly down first edge of first Earflap, **2sc in first of 3 sts at bottom edge, 1sc in next st, 2sc in next st, make 11 sc evenly along other edge of Earflap**, 1sc in each of next 21 sts along front of Hat, make 11 sc evenly along first edge of next Earflap; rep from ** to **, join with a ss in first sc. (89 sts)
Fasten off.

Ears
(make 2)

Round 1: Using MC and US size H/8 (5mm) hook, 2ch, 4sc in second ch from hook. (4 sts)

Round 2: 2sc in each st to end. (8 sts)

Round 3: *1sc in each of next 3 sts, 2sc in next st; rep from * to end. (10 sts)

Round 4: *1sc in each of next 4 sts, 2sc in next st; rep from * to end. (12 sts)

Round 5: *1sc in each of next 5 sts, 2sc in next st; rep from * to end. (14 sts)

Round 6: *1sc in each of next 6 sts, 2sc in next st; rep from * to end. (16 sts)

Round 7: *1sc in each of next 7 sts, 2sc in next st; rep from * to end. (18 sts)

Round 8: *1sc in each of next 8 sts, 2sc in next st; rep from * to end. (20 sts)

Rounds 9–14: 1sc in each st to end. (20 sts)

Ss in next st.

Fasten off leaving a long tail for sewing on.

Sew Ears in place with slight curve toward front.

Muzzle
Work in rounds, placing st marker at beg of each round.

Round 1: Using A and US size E/4 (3.5mm) hook, make 2ch, 6sc in second ch from hook. (6 sts)

Round 2: 2sc in each st to end. (12 sts)

Round 3: *1sc in next st, 2sc in next st; rep from * to end. (18 sts)

Round 4: *1sc in each of next 2 sts, 2sc in next st; rep from * to end. (24 sts)

Round 5: *1sc in each of next 3 sts, 2sc in next st; rep from * to end. (30 sts)

Rounds 6–11: 1sc in each st to end. (30 sts)

Ss in next st.

Fasten off leaving long tail for sewing on.

Blaze
Work in rows.

Using A and US size H/8 (5mm) hook, make 9ch.

Row 1: 1sc in second ch from hook, 1sc in each ch to end. (8 sts)

Rows 2–18: 1ch, 1sc in each st to end.

Fasten off.

Center Muzzle approx 1 row up from bottom edge and pin in place. Pin Blaze in place up center of front of Hat. Sew around edge of Muzzle and Blaze and sew around top of Muzzle using running stitch. When sewing Muzzle, leave gap and stuff lightly. Finish sewing up gap.

Using B, embroider nostrils in satin stitch (see page 18), using the photo as a guide.

Eyes
Using B, embroider eyes in satin stitch (see page 18) approx 8 rows up from bottom edge and 4in (10cm) apart.

Forelock
Using A, cut several strands each approx 6in (15cm). Make tassels with single strands in two rows across top of head above Blaze and between Ears.

Benjamin the badger

Badgers may be nocturnal, but this hat definitely shouldn't be kept in the dark!

Materials

Fyberspates Scrumptious Aran, 55% merino wool, 45% silk worsted (aran) yarn, 3½oz (100g) hank, approx 180yd (165m) per hank:

    1 x hank of shade 405 Slate (gray) (MC)

Debbie Bliss Cashmerino Aran, 55% merino wool, 33% acrylic, 12% cashmere worsted (aran) yarn, 1¾oz (50g) balls, approx 98yd (90m) per ball:

    1 x ball of shade 101 Ecru (off white) (A)
    1 x ball of shade 300 Black (B)
    Small amount of shade 09 Grey (C)

Small amount of black bulky (chunky) yarn

US size H/8 (5mm) and US size E/4 (3.5mm) crochet hooks

Gauge

16 sts x 16 rows over a 4in (10cm) using US size H/8 (5mm) hook, single crochet, and Scrumptious Aran.

Size

To fit age 3–10 years

Finished measurements

Approx 18–20in (46–51cm) circumference, 7in (18cm) high

Abbreviations

approx approximately
beg beginning
ch chain
rep repeat
RS right side
sc single crochet
sc2tog single crochet 2 stitches together
ss slip stitch
st(s) stitch(es)
WS wrong side

Hat

Work in rounds, placing st marker at beg of each round.

Round 1: Using MC and US size H/8 (5mm) hook, 2ch, 6sc in second ch from hook. *(6 sts)*

Round 2: 2sc in each st to end. *(12 sts)*

Round 3: *1sc in next st, 2sc in next st; rep from * to end. *(18 sts)*

Round 4: *1sc in each of next 2 sts, 2sc in next st; rep from * to end. *(24 sts)*

Round 5: *1sc in each of next 3 sts, 2sc in next st; rep from * to end. *(30 sts)*

Round 6: *1sc in each of next 4 sts, 2sc in next st; rep from * to end. *(36 sts)*

Round 7: *1sc in each of next 5 sts, 2sc in next st; rep from * to end. *(42 sts)*

Round 8: *1sc in each of next 6 sts, 2sc in next st; rep from * to end. *(48 sts)*

Round 9: *1sc in each of next 7 sts, 2sc in next st; rep from * to end. *(54 sts)*

Round 10: *1sc in each of next 8 sts, 2sc in next st; rep from * to end. *(60 sts)*

Round 11: *1sc in each of next 9 sts, 2sc in next st; rep from * to end. *(66 sts)*

Rounds 12–29: 1sc in each st to end. *(66 sts)*

Do not fasten off.

First earflap:

1sc in each of next 6 sts. Do not turn.

Work in rows, turning at end of each following row.

Row 1 (RS): 1sc in each of next 15 sts. Turn. *(15 sts)*

Row 2 (WS): 1ch (does not count as st throughout), sc2tog, 1sc in each of next 11 sts, sc2tog. *(13 sts)*

Row 3: 1ch, 1sc in each st to end. *(13 sts)*

Row 4: 1ch, sc2tog, 1sc in each of next 9 sts, sc2tog. *(11 sts)*

Row 5: 1ch, 1sc in each st to end. *(11 sts)*

Row 6: 1ch, sc2tog, 1sc in each of next 7 sts, sc2tog. *(9 sts)*

Row 7: 1ch, 1sc in each st to end. *(9 sts)*

Row 8: 1ch, sc2tog, 1sc in each of next 5 sts, sc2tog. *(7 sts)*

Row 9: 1ch, 1sc in each st to end, sc2tog. *(7 sts)*

Row 10: 1ch, sc2tog, 1sc in each of next 3 sts. *(5 sts)*

Rows 11–16: 1ch, 1sc in each st to end. *(5 sts)*

Fasten off.

Second earflap:

With RS facing, join MC in next st along from end of Row 1 of First earflap.

1ch, 1sc in same st, 1sc in each of next 11 sts, place second st marker here to denote center front of Hat, 1sc in each of next 12 sts. Do not turn. *(24 sts)*

Work in rows, turning at end of each row.

Row 1: 1sc in each of next 15 sts. Turn.

Rep Rows 2–16 of First earflap.

Fasten off.

Ears
(make 2)
Round 1: Using A and US size H/8 (5mm) hook, 2ch, 4sc in second ch from hook. *(4 sts)*
Round 2: 2sc in each st to end. *(8 sts)*
Round 3: *1sc in each of next 3 sts, 2sc in next st; rep from * to end. *(10 sts)*
Round 4: *1sc in each of next 4 sts, 2sc in next st; rep from * to end. *(12 sts)*
Round 5: *1sc n each of next 5 sts, 2sc in next st; rep from * to end. *(14 sts)*
Cut yarn, join B.
Round 6: *1sc in each of next 6 sts, 2sc in next st; rep from * to end. *(16 sts)*
Round 7: *1sc in each of next 7 sts, 2sc in next st; rep from * to end. *(18 sts)*
Round 8: *1sc in each of next 8 sts, 2sc in next st; rep from * to end. *(20 sts)*
Rounds 9–10: 1sc in each st to end. *(20 sts)*
Ss in next st.
Fasten off leaving long tail for sewing on.

Face center stripe
Face is made in three pieces, joined together in rows.
Row 1: Using A and US size H/8 (5mm) hook, make 8ch, 1sc in second ch from hook, 1sc in each st to end. *(6 sts)*
Row 2: 1ch, 1sc in each st to end.
Rep Row 2 another 25 times.
Fasten off.

Face side 1
Row 1 (RS): Using B and US size H/8 (5mm) hook, make 12ch, 1sc in second ch from hook, 1sc in each st to end. *(11 sts)*
Row 2 (WS): 1ch (does not count as st throughout), 1sc in each st to end. *(11 sts)*
Row 3 (RS): 1ch, 1sc in each st to last 2 sts, sc2tog. *(10 sts)*
Row 4 (WS): 1ch, 1sc in each st to end. *(10 sts)*
Row 5 (RS): 1ch, 1sc in each st to last 2 sts, sc2tog. *(9 sts)*
Rows 6–7: 1ch, 1sc in each st to end. *(9 sts)*
Row 8 (WS): 1ch, sc2tog, 1sc in each st to end. *(8 sts)*
Rows 9–10: 1ch, 1sc in each st to end. *(8 sts)*
Row 11 (RS): 1ch, 1sc in each st to last 2 sts, sc2tog. *(7 sts)*
Rows 12–13: 1ch, 1sc in each st to end. *(7 sts)*
Row 14 (WS): 1ch, sc2tog, 1sc in each st to end. *(6 sts)*
Rows 15–16: 1ch, 1sc in each st to end. *(6 sts)*
Row 17 (RS): 1ch, 1sc in each st to last 2 sts, sc2tog. *(5 sts)*
Rows 18–19: 1ch, 1sc in each st to end. *(5 sts)*
Row 20 (WS): 1ch, sc2tog, 1sc in each st to end. *(4 sts)*
Rows 21–22: 1ch, 1sc in each st to end. *(4 sts)*
Row 23 (RS): 1ch, 1sc in each st to last 2 sts, sc2tog. *(3 sts)*
Row 24 (WS): 1ch, 1sc in each st to end. *(3 sts)*
Row 25 (RS): 1ch, 1sc in first st, sc2tog. *(2 sts)*
Row 26 (WS): 1ch, sc2tog. *(1 st)*
Fasten off, leaving long tail for sewing up.

Face side 2
Row 1 (RS): Using B and US size H/8 (5mm) hook, make 12ch, 1sc in second ch from hook, 1sc in each st to end. *(11 sts)*
Row 2 (WS): 1ch (does not count as st throughout), 1sc in each st to end. *(11 sts)*
Row 3 (RS): 1ch, sc2tog, 1sc in each st to end. *(10 sts)*

Row 4 (WS): 1ch, 1sc in each st to end. *(10 sts)*
Row 5 (RS): 1ch, sc2tog, 1sc in each st end. *(9 sts)*
Rows 6–7: 1ch, 1sc in each st to end. *(9 sts)*
Row 8 (WS): 1ch, 1sc in each st to end, sc2tog *(8 sts)*
Rows 9–10: 1ch, 1sc in each st to end. *(8 sts)*
Row 11 (RS): 1ch, sc2tog, 1sc in each st to end. *(7 sts)*
Rows 12–13: 1ch, 1sc in each st to end. *(7 sts)*
Row 14 (WS): 1ch, 1sc in each st to last 2 sts, sc2tog. *(6 sts)*
Rows 15–16: 1ch, 1sc in each st to end. *(6 sts)*
Row 17 (RS): 1ch, sc2tog, 1sc in each st end. *(5 sts)*
Rows 18–19: 1ch, 1sc in each st to end. *(5 sts)*
Row 20 (WS): 1ch, 1sc in each st to last 2 sts, sc2tog. *(4 sts)*
Rows 21–22: 1ch, 1sc in each st to end. *(4 sts)*
Row 23 (RS): 1ch, sc2tog, 1sc in each st to end. *(3 sts)*
Row 24 (WS): 1ch, 1sc in each st to end. *(3 sts)*
Row 25 (RS): 1ch, sc2tog, 1sc in last st. *(2 sts)*
Row 26 (WS): 1ch, sc2tog. *(1 st)*
Fasten off leaving long tail for sewing up.

With RS together, sew straight edges of Sides to each side of
Center Stripe.
Place st marker in center stitch of Face Center Stripe, at end
where Side pieces are most narrow.
With WS of Face to RS front of Hat, match both markers
together. Pin and sew Face onto front of Hat using B.

Ears and eyes
Sew an Ear on top of each Face Side.
Using C and B, embroider eyes in satin stitch (see page 18),
using the photo as a guide.
Add pupils using French knots (see page 19), using black
bulky (chunky) yarn.

Nose
Work in rounds, placing st marker at beg of each round.
Round 1: Using B and US size E/4 (3.5mm) hook, make 2ch,
6sc in second ch from hook. *(6 sts)*
Round 2: 2sc in each st to end. *(12 sts)*
Round 3: *1sc in next st, 2sc in next st; rep from * to end.
(18 sts)
Rounds 4–6: 1sc in each st to end.
Ss in next st.
Fasten off leaving a long tail for sewing on.

Lightly stuff Nose using ends from other pieces.
Pin Nose to bottom edge of center of Face and sew in place.

A really fabulous dog breed—I had a Collie for 18 years, so this is a project dear to my heart.

Monty the border collie

Materials
Debbie Bliss Cashmerino Aran, 55% merino wool, 33% acrylic, 12% cashmere worsted (aran) yarn, 1¾oz (50g) balls, approx 98yd (90m) per ball:
  2 x balls of shade 300 Black (MC)
  1 x ball of shade 025 White (A):

Small amount of brown light worsted (DK) yarn (B)

US size H/8 (5mm) and US size E/4 (3.5mm) crochet hooks

Yarn sewing needle

Small amount of polyester toy stuffing

Gauge
16 sts x 16 rows over a 4in (10cm) square using US size H/8 (5mm) hook, single crochet, and Cashmerino Aran.

Size
To fit age 3–10 years

Finished measurements
Approx 18–20in (46–51cm) circumference, 7in (18cm) high

Abbreviations
approx approximately
beg begin(ning)
ch chain
rep repeat
RS right side
sc single crochet
sc2tog single crochet 2 stitches together
ss slip stitch
st(s) stitch(es)
WS wrong side

Hat
Work in rounds, placing st marker at beg of each round.

Round 1: Using MC and US size H/8 (5mm) hook, 2ch, 6sc in second ch from hook. (*6 sts*)

Round 2: 2sc in each st to end. (*12 sts*)

Round 3: *1sc in next st, 2sc in next st; rep from * to end. (*18 sts*)

Round 4: *1sc in each of next 2 sts, 2sc in next st; rep from * to end. (*24 sts*)

Round 5: *1sc in each of next 3 sts, 2sc in next st; rep from * to end. (*30 sts*)

Round 6: *1sc in each of next 4 sts, 2sc in next st; rep from * to end. (*36 sts*)

Round 7: *1sc in each of next 5 sts, 2sc in next st; rep from * to end. (*42 sts*)

Round 8: *1sc in each of next 6 sts, 2sc in next st; rep from * to end. (*48 sts*)

Round 9: *1sc in each of next 7 sts, 2sc in next st; rep from * to end. (*54 sts*)

Round 10: *1sc in each of next 8 sts, 2sc in next st; rep from * to end. (*60 sts*)

Round 11: *1sc in each of next 9 sts, 2sc in next st; rep from * to end. (*66 sts*)

Rounds 12–28: 1sc in each st to end. (*66 sts*)

Do not fasten off.

Place first st marker here to denote center back of Hat.

First earflap:

1sc in each of next 6 sts. Do not turn.

Beg working in rows, turning at end of each following row.

Row 1 (RS): 1sc in each of next 15 sts. Turn. *(15 sts)*

Row 2 (WS): 1ch (does not count as st throughout), sc2tog,1sc in each of next 11 sts, sc2tog. *(13 sts)*

Row 3: 1ch, 1sc in each st to end. *(13 sts)*

Row 4: 1ch, sc2tog, 1sc in each of next 9 sts, sc2tog. *(11 sts)*

Row 5: 1ch, 1sc in each st to end. *(11 sts)*

Row 6: 1ch, sc2tog, 1sc in each of next 7 sts, sc2tog. *(9 sts)*

Row 7: 1ch, 1sc in each st to end. *(9 sts)*

Row 8: 1ch, sc2tog, 1sc in each of next 5 sts, sc2tog. *(7 sts)*

Row 9: 1ch, 1sc in each st to end. *(7 sts)*

Row 10: 1ch, sc2tog, 1sc in each of next 3 sts, sc2tog. *(5 sts)*

Row 11: 1ch, 1sc in each st to end. *(5 sts)*

Row 12: 1ch, sc2tog, 1sc in next st, sc2tog. *(3 sts)*

Rows 13–14: 1ch, 1sc in each st to end. *(3 sts)*

Fasten off.

Second earflap:

With RS facing, join MC in next st along from end of Row 1 of First earflap.

1ch, 1sc in same st, 1sc in each of next 11 sts, place second st marker here to denote center front of Hat, 1sc in each of next 12 sts. Do not turn. *(24 sts)*

Work in rows, turning at end of each following row.

Row 1: 1sc in each of next 15 sts. Turn.

Rep Rows 2–14 of First earflap.

Edging:

With RS of work facing, rejoin MC at back of work at start of straight edging after Earflap.

1ch, 1sc in same st, 1sc in each of next 11 sts along back of Hat to start of Earflap.

Make 12 sc evenly down first edge of first Earflap.

2sc in first of 3 sts at bottom edge, 1sc in next st, 2sc in next st, make 12 sc evenly along other edge of Earflap, 1sc in each of next 24 sts along front of Hat,make 12 sc evenly along first edge of next Earflap; rep from ** to **, join with ss in first sc. *(94 sts)*

Fasten off.

Muzzle

Work in rounds, placing st marker at beg of each round.

Round 1: Using A and US size E/4 (3.5mm) hook, make 2ch, 6sc in second ch from hook. *(6 sts)*

Round 2: 2sc in each st to end. *(12 sts)*

Round 3: *1sc in next st, 2sc in next st; rep from * to end. *(18 sts)*

Round 4: *1sc in each of next 2 sts, 2sc in next st; rep from * to end. *(24 sts)*

Rounds 5–8: 1sc in each st to end.

Ss in next st.

Fasten off.

Nose

Work in rows, turning at end of each row.

Row 1: Using A and US size E/4 (3.5mm) hook, make 2ch, 3sc in second ch from hook. Turn.

Row 2: 1ch, 2sc in first st, 1sc in next st, 2sc in last st. *(5 sts)*

Row 3: 1ch, 1sc in each st to end. *(5 sts)*

Row 4: 1ch, 2sc in first st, 1sc in each of next 3 sts, 2sc in last st. *(7 sts)*

Row 5: 1ch, 1sc in each st to end. *(7 sts)*

Fasten off, leaving a long tail for sewing onto Muzzle.

Using long tail, sew Nose to Muzzle and embroider the mouth using backstitch.

Stuff Muzzle lightly and sew onto front of Hat at bottom edge.

Ears

(make 2)

Round 1: Using MC and US size H/8 (5mm) hook, 2ch, 4sc in second ch from hook. *(4 sts)*

Round 2: 2sc in each st to end. *(8 sts)*

Round 3: *1sc in each of next 3 sts, 2sc in next st; rep from * once more. *(10 sts)*

Round 4: *1sc in each of next 4 sts, 2sc in next st; rep from * once more. *(12 sts)*

Round 5: *1sc in each of next 5 sts, 2sc in next st; rep from * once more. *(14 sts)*

Round 6: *1sc in each of next 6 sts, 2sc in next st; rep from * once more. *(16 sts)*

Round 7: *1sc in each of next 7 sts, 2sc in next st; rep from * once more. *(18 sts)*

Round 8: *1sc in each of next 8 sts, 2sc in next st; rep from * once more. *(20 sts)*

Rounds 9–11: 1sc in each st to end. *(20 sts)*

Ss in next st.

Fasten off, leaving a long tail for sewing on.

Sew Ears in place at top of Hat at center approx 3in (7.5cm) apart.

Stripe

Row 1: Using A and US size E/4 (3.5mm) hook and B, make 5ch, 1sc in second ch from hook, 1sc in each of next 3 sts. *(4 sts)*

Row 2: 1ch, 1sc in each st to end. *(4 sts)*

Rep Row 2 until work measures approx 3½in (9cm) or until the length is from the top of the Muzzle to 2 rows from the top.

Next row: 1ch, 2sc in first st, 1sc in each of next 2 sts, 2sc in last st. *(6 sts)*

Next row: 1ch, 1sc in each st to end.

Fasten off leaving a long tail for sewing on.

Center Stripe on front of Hat vertically, from top of Muzzle to top of Hat and with widest part of Stripe at Muzzle. Sew on using long tail.

Eyes

Using scraps of MC and B, embroider eyes in satin stitch (see page 18) and pupils using French knots (see page 19) approx three rows above Muzzle and 3 sts either side of Stripe, using the photo as a guide.

Karl the sheep

A hat that will keep you super warm! This is made using a loop stitch, which is easy once you get the hang of it.

Materials
Debbie Bliss Cashmerino Aran, 55% merino wool, 33% acrylic, 12% cashmere worsted (aran) yarn, 1¾oz (50g) balls, approx 98yd (90m) per ball:

    1 x ball of shade 025 White (A)
    1 x ball of shade 300 Black (B)
    1 x ball of shade 603 Baby Pink (pink) (C)

US size H/8 (5mm) and US size E/4 (3.5mm) crochet hooks

Yarn sewing needle

9mm black safety eyes

Gauge
16 sts x 16 rows over a 4in (10cm) square using US size H/8 (5mm) hook, single crochet, and Cashmerino Aran.

Size
To fit age 3–10 years

Finished measurements
Approx 18–20in (46–51cm) circumference, 7in (18cm) high

Abbreviations
approx approximately
beg beginning
ch chain
rep repeat
RS right side
sc single crochet
sc2tog single crochet 2 stitches together
ss slip stitch
st(s) stitch(es)
WS wrong side

Special abbreviation
Loop St—with yarn over left index finger, insert hook in next st, draw 2 strands through st (take first strand from under index finger and at same time take second strand from over index finger) pull yarn to tighten loop forming a 1in (2.5cm) loop on index finger. Remove finger from loop, put loop to back (WS) of work, yoh and pull through 3 loops on hook (1 Loop St made on WS of work).

Hat
Work in rounds, placing st marker at beg of each round.
Round 1: Using A and US size H/8 (5mm) hook, 2ch, 6sc in second ch from hook. *(6 sts)*
Round 2: 2sc in each st to end. *(12 sts)*
Use Loop St in each st for following rounds:
Round 3: *1sc in next st, 2sc in next st; rep from * to end. *(18 sts)*
Round 4: *1sc in each of next 2 sts, 2sc in next st; rep from * to end. *(24 sts)*
Round 5: *1sc in each of next 3 sts, 2sc in next st; rep from * to end. *(30 sts)*
Round 6: *1sc in each of next 4 sts, 2sc in next st; rep from * to end. *(36 sts)*
Round 7: *1sc in each of next 5 sts, 2sc in next st; rep from * to end. *(42 sts)*
Round 8: *1sc in each of next 6 sts, 2sc in next st; rep from * to end. *(48 sts)*
Round 9: *1sc in each of next 7 sts, 2sc in next st; rep from * to end. *(54 sts)*
Round 10: *1sc in each of next 8 sts, 2sc in next st; rep from * to end. *(60 sts)*
Round 11: *1sc in each of next 9 sts, 2sc in next st; rep from * to end. Cut yarn, do not fasten off. *(66 sts)*

Rounds 12–26: Join B, 1sc in each st to end. *(66 sts)*
Do not fasten off.
Place first st marker here to denote center back of Hat.

First earflap:
Using B, 1sc in each of next 6 sts. Do not turn.
Beg working in rows, turning at end of each following row.
Row 1 (RS): 1sc in each of next 15 sts. Turn. *(15 sts)*
Row 2 (WS): 1ch (does not count as st throughout), sc2tog, 1sc in each of next 11 sts, sc2tog. *(13 sts)*
Row 3: 1ch, 1sc in each st to end. *(13 sts)*
Row 4: 1ch, sc2tog, 1sc in each of next 9 sts, sc2tog. *(11 sts)*
Row 5: 1ch, 1sc in each st to end. *(11 sts)*
Row 6: 1ch, sc2tog, 1sc in each of next 7 sts, sc2tog. *(9 sts)*
Row 7: 1ch, 1sc in each st to end. *(9 sts)*
Row 8: 1ch, sc2tog, 1sc in each of next 5 sts, sc2tog. *(7 sts)*
Row 9: 1ch, 1sc in each st to end. *(7 sts)*
Row 10: 1ch, sc2tog, 1sc in each of next 3 sts, sc2tog. *(5 sts)*
Row 11: 1ch, 1sc in each st to end. *(5 sts)*
Row 12: 1ch, sc2tog, 1sc in next st, sc2tog. *(3 sts)*
Row 13: 1ch, 1sc in each st to end. *(3 sts)*
Fasten off.

Second earflap:
With RS facing, join B in next st along from end of Row 1 of First earflap.
1ch, 1sc in same st, 1sc in each of next 11 sts, place second st marker here to denote center front of Hat, 1sc in each of next 12 sts. Do not turn. *(24 sts)*
Work in rows, turning at end of each following row.
Row 1: 1sc in each of next 15 sts. Turn.
Rep Rows 2–13 of First earflap.

Edging:
With RS of work facing, rejoin B at back of work at start of straight edging after second Earflap. 1ch, 1sc in same st, 1sc in each of next 11 sts along back of Hat to start of Earflap.
Make 12sc evenly down first edge of first Earflap.
2sc in first st of 3 sts at bottom edge, 1sc in next st, 2sc in next st, make 12sc evenly along other edge of Earflap, 1sc in each of next 24 sts along front of Hat, make 12sc evenly along first edge of next Earflap; rep from ** to **, join with a ss in first sc. *(94 sts)*
Fasten off.

Outer ear

(make 2)
Work in rows, turning at end of each row.
Row 1: Using A and US size E/4 (3.5mm) hook, make 2ch, 3sc in second ch from hook. Turn. *(3 sts)*
Row 2: 1ch (does not count as st throughout), 2sc in first st, 1sc in next st, 2sc in last st. *(5 sts)*
Row 3: 1ch, 1sc in each st to end. *(5 sts)*
Row 4: 1ch, 2sc in first st, 1sc in each of next 3 sts, 2sc in last st. *(7 sts)*
Row 5: 1ch, 1sc in each st to end. *(7 sts)*
Row 6: 1ch, 2sc in first st, 1sc in each of next 5 sts, 2sc in last st. *(9 sts)*
Row 7: 1ch, 1sc in each st to end. *(9 sts)*
Row 8: 1ch, 2sc in first st, 1sc in each of next 7 sts, 2sc in last st. *(11 sts)*
Row 9: 1ch, 1sc in each st to end. *(11 sts)*
Row 10: 1ch, 2sc in first st, 1sc in each of next 9 sts, 2sc in last st. *(13 sts)*
Rows 11–19: 1ch, 1sc in each st to end. *(13 sts)*
Fasten off, leaving a long tail for sewing Inner ear to Outer ear.

Inner ear

(make 2)

Work in rows, turning at end of each row.

Row 1: Using C and US size E/4 (3.5mm) hook, make 2ch, 3sc in second ch from hook. Turn. *(3 sts)*

Row 2: 1ch, 2sc in first st, 1sc in next st, 2sc in last st. *(5 sts)*

Rows 3–4: 1ch, 1sc in each st to end. *(5 sts)*

Row 5: 1ch, 2sc in first st, 1sc in each of next 3 sts, 2sc in last st. *(7 sts)*

Rows 6–7: 1ch, 1sc in each st to end. *(7 sts)*

Row 8: 1ch, 2sc in first st, 1sc in each of next 5 sts, 2sc in last st. *(9 sts)*

Rows 9–19: 1ch, 1sc in each st to end. *(9 sts)*

Fasten off.

With RS together, pin and sew outside edges of Inner ear and Outer ear together leaving bottom edge open. Turn RS out. Position ears on top of Hat, approx 7in (18cm) apart spanning Rows 9–11. Shape outer edges of ears towards middle, and pin and sew in place.

Eyes

(make 2)

Work in rounds, placing st marker at beg of each round.

Using A and US size E/4 (3.5mm) hook, and leaving a long tail of approx 6in (15cm), make 2ch, make 6sc into second ch from hook.

Round 1 (RS): 1ch (does not count as st throughout), 1sc in first st, 2sc in each of next 5 sts, join with ss in first sc. *(11 sts)*

Round 2: 1ch, 1sc in each st to end, join with ss in first sc. *(11 sts)*

Round 3: 1ch, skip first st, sc2tog around, join with ss in first sc.

Fasten off leaving a long tail.

Sew in ends but do not cut tails.

Keeping Eyes RS out, insert safety eye into center of each Eye. Use one yarn tail to stuff center of Eye and other other tail to sew onto Hat approx 9 rows from bottom edge and 3 sts apart.

A really fun, bright kitty, and this is a good way to use up scraps of wool to make the stripes.

Jonathan the rainbow cat

Materials

Debbie Bliss Cashmerino Aran, 55% merino wool, 33% acrylic, 12% cashmere worsted (aran) yarn, 1¾oz (50g) balls, approx 98yd (90m) per ball:

    1 x ball of shade 101 Ecru (off white) (A)
    1 x ball of shade 048 Burnt Orange (orange) (B)
    1 x ball of shade 062 Kingfisher (dark blue) (C)
    1 x ball of shade 047 Aqua (light blue) (D)
    1 x ball of shade 610 Ruby (red) (E)
    1 x ball of shade 077 Gold (yellow) (F)
    1 x ball of shade 502 Lime (green) (G)

Small amounts of black yarn (eyes) and brown yarn (mouth)

US size H/8 (5mm) crochet hook

Yarn sewing needle

Gauge

16 sts x 16 rows over a 4in (10cm) square using US size H/8 (5mm) hook, single crochet, and Cashmerino Aran.

Size

To fit age 3–10 years

Finished measurements

Approx 18–20in (46–51cm) circumference, 7in (18cm) high

Abbreviations

approx approximately
beg begin(ning)
ch chain
rep repeat
RS right side
sc single crochet
sc2tog single crochet 2 stitches together
ss slip stitch
st(s) stitch(es)
WS wrong side

Hat

Work in rounds, placing st marker at beg of each round.

Round 1: Using A, 2ch, 6sc in second ch from hook. (*6 sts*)

Round 2: 2sc in each st to end. (*12 sts*)

Round 3: *1sc in next st, 2sc in next st; rep from * to end. (*18 sts*)

Round 4: 1sc in each of next 2 sts, 2sc in next st; rep from * to end. (*24 sts*)

Round 5: *1sc in each of next 3 sts, 2sc in next st; rep from * to end. (*30 sts*)

Round 6: *1sc in each of next 4 sts, 2sc in next st; rep from * to end. (*36 sts*)

Round 7: *1sc in each of next 5 sts, 2sc in next st; rep from * to end. (*42 sts*)

Round 8: *1sc in each of next 6 sts, 2sc in next st; rep from * to end. (*48 sts*)

Round 9: *1sc in each of next 7 sts, 2sc in next st; rep from * to end. (*54 sts*)

Round 10: *1sc in each of next 8 sts, 2sc in next st; rep from * to end. (*60 sts*)

Round 11: *1sc in each of next 9 sts, 2sc in next st; rep from * to end. (*66 sts*)

Rounds 12–17: 1sc in each st to end. (*66 sts*)

Cut yarn, do not fasten off.

Rounds 18–19: Join B, 1sc in each st to end. Cut yarn, do not fasten off.

Rounds 20–21: Join C, 1sc in each st to end. Cut yarn, do not fasten off.

Rounds 22–23: Join D, 1sc in each st to end. Cut yarn, do not fasten off.

Rounds 24–25: Join E, 1sc in each st to end. Cut yarn, do not fasten off.

Rounds 26–27: Join F, 1sc in each st to end. Cut yarn, do not fasten off.

Rounds 28–29: Join G, 1sc in each st to end. Do not fasten off.

Place first st marker here to denote back of Hat.

First earflap:

Join A, 1sc in each of next 6 sts. Do not turn.

Beg working in rows, turning at end of each following row.

Row 1 (RS): 1sc in each of next 15 sts. Turn. (*15 sts*)

Row 2 (WS): 1ch, sc2tog, 1sc in each of next 11 sts, sc2tog. (*13 sts*)

Row 3: 1ch, 1sc in each st to end. (*13 sts*)

Row 4: 1ch, sc2tog, 1sc in each of next 9 sts, sc2tog. (*11 sts*)

Row 5: 1ch, 1sc in each st to end. (*11 sts*)

Row 6: 1ch, sc2tog, 1sc in each of next 7 sts, sc2tog. *(9 sts)*
Row 7: 1ch, 1sc in each st to end. *(9 sts)*
Row 8: 1ch, sc2tog, 1sc in each of next 5 sts, sc2tog. *(7 sts)*
Row 9: 1ch, 1sc in each st to end. *(7 sts)*
Row 10: 1ch, sc2tog, 1sc in each of next 3 sts, sc2tog. *(5 sts)*
Row 11: 1ch, 1sc in each st to end. *(5 sts)*
Row 12: 1ch, sc2tog, 1sc in next st, sc2tog. *(3 sts)*
Row 13: 1ch, 1sc in each st to end. *(3 sts)*
Fasten off.

Second earflap:
With RS facing, join A in next st along from end of Row 1 of First earflap.
1ch, 1sc in same st, 1sc in each of next 11 sts, place second st marker here to denote front of hat, 1sc in each of next 12 sts. Do not turn. *(24 sts)*
Work in rows, turning at end of each following row.
Row 1: 1sc in each of next 15 sts. Turn.
Rep Rows 2–13 of First Earflap.

Edging:
With RS of work facing, rejoin A at back of work at start of straight edging after Second earflap.
1ch, 1sc in same st, 1sc in each of next 11 sts along back of Hat to start of Earflap.
Make 12sc evenly down first edge of first Earflap.
2sc in first st of three sts at bottom edge, 1sc in next st, 2sc in next st, make 12sc evenly along other edge of Earflap,
1sc in each of next 24 sts along Front of Hat, make 12sc evenly along first edge of next Earflap; rep from ** to **, join with a ss in first sc. *(94 sts)*
Fasten off.

Ears
(make 2)
Work in rounds, placing st marker at beg of each round.
Round 1: Using A and US size H/8 (5mm) hook, 2ch, 4sc in second ch from hook. *(4 sts)*
Round 2: 2sc in each st to end. *(8 sts)*
Round 3: *1sc in each of next 3 sts, 2sc in next st; rep from * to end. *(10 sts)*
Round 4: *1sc in each of next 4 sts, 2sc in next st; rep from * to end. *(12 sts)*
Round 5: *1sc n each of next 5 sts, 2sc in next st; rep from * to end. *(14 sts)*
Round 6: *1sc in each of next 6 sts, 2sc in next st; rep from * to end. *(16 sts)*
Round 7: *1sc in each of next 7 sts, 2sc in next st; rep from * to end. *(18 sts)*
Round 8: *1sc in each of next 8 sts, 2sc in next st; rep from * to end. *(20 sts)*
Rounds 9–11: 1sc in each st to end. *(20 sts)*
Ss in next st.
Fasten off, leaving long tail for sewing on.
Sew Ears onto top of Hat.

Sew in end from starting point.
With ears flat and using long tail, sew onto hat approx 3in (7.5cm) apart and starting 4 rows down from top.
Using black yarn, embroider eyes in satin stitch (see page 18).
Using brown yarn, embroider mouth in straight stitch (see page 18).

Gobbie the shark

The sharp teeth really make this shark look fierce, but if you want to make a friendlier shark, just do away with the teeth and the gums.

Materials
Debbie Bliss Cashmerino Aran, 55% merino wool, 33% acrylic, 12% cashmere worsted (aran) yarn, 1¾oz (50g) balls, approx 98yd (90m) per ball:
   1 x ball of shade 009 Grey (MC)
   1 x ball of shade 025 White (B)

Debbie Bliss Rialto DK, 100% merino wool light worsted (DK) yarn, 1¾oz (50g) balls, approx 115yd (105m) per ball:
   Small amount of shade 012 Scarlet (A)

US size H/8 (5mm) and US size E/4 (3.5mm) crochet hooks

Yarn sewing needle

9mm black safety eyes

Gauge
15 sts x 11 rows over a 4in (10cm) square using US size H/8 (5mm) hook, half double crochet, and Cashmerino Aran.

Size
To fit age 3–10 years

Finished measurements
Approx 18–20in (46–51cm) circumference, 7in (18cm) high

Abbreviations
approx approximately
beg beginning
ch chain
dc double crochet
hdc half double crochet
rep repeat
RS right side
sc single crochet
sc2tog single crochet 2 stitches together
ss slip stitch
st(s) stitch(es)
WS wrong side

Hat
Work in rounds, placing st marker at beg of each round.
Round 1: Using MC and US size H/8 (5mm) hook, make 2ch, 4hdc in second ch from hook. (*4 sts*)
Round 2: 2hdc in each st to end. (*8 sts*)
Round 3: Rep Round 2. (*16 sts*)
Round 4: *1hdc in next st, 2hdc in next st; rep from * to end. (*24 sts*)
Round 5: *1hdc in each of next 2 sts, 2hdc in next st; rep from * to end. (*32 sts*)
Round 6: *1hdc in each of next 3 sts, 2hdc in next st; rep from * to end. (*40 sts*)
Round 7: *1hdc in each of next 4 sts, 2hdc in next st; rep from * to end. (*48 sts*)

Round 8: *1hdc in each of next 5 sts, 2hdc in next st; rep from * to end. (*56 sts*)
Round 9: *1hdc in each of next 6 sts, 2hdc in next st; rep from * to end. (*64 sts*)
Round 10: *1hdc in each of next 7 sts, 2hdc in next st; rep from * to end. (*72 sts*)
Rounds 11–22: 1hdc in each st to end, or until work measures approx 7in (18cm) from start. (*72 sts*)
Next round: 1sc in each st to end, ss in last st. (*72 sts*)
Do not fasten off.
Do not remove st marker as this marks center back of Hat.

Dorsal fin

Row 1: Using MC and US size H/8 (5mm) hook, leave a long starting tail, make 2ch, 4sc in second ch from hook. (*4 sts*)

Row 2: 1ch (does not count as st throughout), 2sc in each st to end. (*8 sts*)

Row 3: 1ch, 1sc in each of next 2 st, 2dc in each of next 4 sts, 1sc in each of next 2 sts. (*12 sts*)

Row 4: 2ch, 3dc in first st, 2dc in next st, 1dc in next st, 2dc in next st, 1dc in each of next 4 sts, 2dc in next st, 1dc in next st, 2dc in next st, 3dc in last st. (*20 sts*)

Row 5: 2ch, [2dc in next st, 1dc in next st] 5 times, [1dc in next st, 2dc in next st] 5 times. (*30 sts*)

Do not fasten off.

Draw up loop and take hook out. Fold piece in half with WS together, put hook back in and pull yarn to secure loop on hook, make ss across curved seam to join two halves. Fasten off, leaving a long tail to sew onto top of Hat. Using starting tail, sew straight edges of two halves of back of Dorsal fin together.

Tail

(*make 2*)

Row 1: Using MC and US size H/8 (5mm) hook, 16ch, make 1sc in second ch from hook, 1sc in each of next 2 ch, 1hdc in each of next 3 ch, 1dc in each of next 3 ch, 2dc in each of next 2 ch, 1dc in next ch, 1hdc in next ch, 1sc in each of next 2 ch.

Row 2: 1ch, 1sc in each of next 2 sts, 1hdc in each of next 2 sts, 1dc in next st, [1dc, 1ch, 1dc] in each of next 2 sts, 1dc in each of next 2 sts, 1hdc in each of next 3 sts, 1sc in each of next 5 sts.

Fasten off.

Sew in both ends of first piece. Sew in starting yarn end only of second piece. Using finishing yarn end of second piece, place pieces WS together and join using ss evenly around all sides.
Sew curved end of Tail onto Hat approx 5 rows from center back marker at bottom edge, with longer part of Tail towards top.
Sew Dorsal fin onto top of Hat with curve facing to front of Hat in line with tail.

Teeth and gums

Gums:

Using front of Dorsal fin as marker, fold Hat in half and place a st marker in center bottom edge to mark center of front of Hat.
Place st markers 12 sts to left and right of central st marker.
With RS facing, join A in back of st with right st marker.
Working in back loops only and using US size E/4 (3.5mm) hook, 1ch, 1sc in same st, 1sc in each st of next 25 sts.
Fasten off, but do not turn.

Teeth:

Working in front loops only and using US size E/4 (3.5mm) hook, join B in same sc of MC of previous row, where Gums have been worked. *4ch, 1sc in second ch from hook, 1hdc in next ch, 1dc in next ch, skip 2 sts, 1sc in next ch; rep from * to end of gums, ss in last st. (*8 teeth*)

Fasten off.

Eyes

(*make 2*)

Work in rounds, placing st marker at beg of each round.
Using B and US size E/4 (3.5mm) hook, and leaving a long tail of approx 6in (15cm), make 2ch, make 5sc into second ch from hook, join with ss to form a ring. (*5 sts*)

Round 1 (RS): 1ch (does not count as st throughout), 1sc in first st, 2sc in each of next 4 sts, join with ss in first sc. (*9 sts*)

Round 2: 1ch, 1sc in each st to end, join with ss in first sc. (*9 sts*)

Round 3: 1ch, skip first st, sc2tog around, join with ss in first sc.
Fasten off leaving a long tail.

Sew in ends but do not cut tails.
Keeping Eyes RS out, insert safety eye into center of each Eye.
Use one of yarn tails to stuff center of Eye and other tail to sew onto Hat approx 4 rows from bottom edge and 10 sts apart.

A ginger burglar cat in disguise. This is a really easy hat, with little detail on the face, but it's still a very fun project.

Ronnie the burglar cat

Materials

Debbie Bliss Falkland Aran, 100% wool worsted (aran) yarn, 3½oz (100g) hanks, approx 197yd (180m) per hank:

  1 x hank of shade 06 Ginger (orange) (MC)
  1 x hank of shade 02 Black (A)

Debbie Bliss Cashmerino Aran, 55% merino wool, 33% acrylic, 12% cashmere worsted (aran) yarn, 1¾oz (50g) balls, approx 98yd (90m) per ball:

  1 x ball of shade 025 White (B)

US size H/8 (5mm) and US size E/4 (3.5mm) crochet hooks

Yarn sewing needle

Gauge

15 sts x 11 rows over a 4in (10cm) square using US size H/8 (5mm) hook, half double crochet, and Falkland Aran.

Size

To fit age 3–10 years

Finished measurements

Approx 18–20in (46–51cm) circumference, 7in (18cm) high

Abbreviations

approx approximately
beg beginning
ch chain
hdc half double crochet
rep repeat
sc single crochet
ss slip stitch
st(s) stitch(es)

Hat

Work in rounds, placing st marker at beg of each round.

Round 1: Using MC and US size H/8 (5mm) hook, make 2ch, 4hdc in second ch from hook. *(4 sts)*

Round 2: 2hdc in each st to end. *(8 sts)*

Round 3: Rep Round 2. *(16 sts)*

Round 4: *1hdc in next st, 2hdc in next st; rep from * to end. *(24 sts)*

Round 5: *1hdc in each of next 2 sts, 2hdc in next st; rep from * to end. *(32 sts)*

Round 6: *1hdc in each of next 3 sts, 2hdc in next st; rep from * to end. *(40 sts)*

Round 7: *1hdc in each of next 4 sts, 2hdc in next st; rep from * to end. *(48 sts)*

Round 8: *1hdc in each of next 5 sts, 2hdc in next st; rep from * to end. *(56 sts)*

Round 9: *1hdc in each of next 6 sts, 2hdc in next st; rep from * to end. *(64 sts)*

Round 10: *1hdc in each of next 7 sts, 2hdc in next st; rep from * to end. Cut yarn, do not fasten off. *(72 sts)*

Rounds 11–16: Join A, 1sc in each st to end. Cut yarn, do not fasten off. *(72 sts)*

Rounds 17–22: Join MC, 1hdc in each st to end. *(72 sts)*

Round 23: 1sc in each st to end. *(72 sts)*

Ss in next st.

Fasten off.

Eyes

(make 2)

Round 1: Using B and US size E/4 (3.5mm) hook, make 2ch, 6sc in second ch from hook. *(6 sts)*

Round 2: 2sc in each st to end. *(12 sts)*

Ss in next st.

Fasten off.

Using A, embroider pupils in satin stitch (see page 18) in center of eyes.

Sew Eyes approx 8 sts apart onto front of Hat in center of black band.

Ears

(make 2)

Work in rounds, placing st marker at beg of each round.

Round 1: Using MC and US size E/4 (3.5mm) hook, 2ch, 4sc in second ch from hook. *(4 sts)*

Round 2: 2sc in each st to end. *(8 sts)*

Round 3: *1sc in each of next 3 sts, 2sc in next st; rep from * to end. *(10 sts)*

Round 4: *1sc in each of next 4 sts, 2sc in next st; rep from * to end. *(12 sts)*

Round 5: *1sc in each of next 5 sts, 2sc in next st; rep from * to end. *(14 sts)*

Round 6: *1sc in each of next 6 sts, 2sc in next st; rep from * to end. *(16 sts)*

Round 7: *1sc in each of next 7 sts, 2sc in next st; rep from * to end. *(18 sts)*

Round 8: *1sc in each of next 8 sts, 2sc in next st; rep from * to end. *(20 sts)*

Rounds 9–10: 1sc in each st to end. *(20 sts)*

Ss in next st.

Fasten off, leaving long tail for sewing on.

Sew Ears onto top of Hat starting approx 3 rows down and 2½in (6cm) apart.

chapter 3
fun hats for the young at heart

There's lots of detail on this hat but it's tremendous fun to make and wear.

Domingo the cockerel

Materials
Debbie Bliss Cashmerino Aran, 55% merino wool, 33% acrylic, 12% cashmere worsted (aran) yarn, 1¾oz (50g) balls, approx 98yd (90m) per ball:
   2 x balls of shade 025 White (MC)
   1 x ball each of shade 610 Ruby (deep red) (A) and shade 064 Cowslip (yellow) (B)

Debbie Bliss Baby Cashmerino, 55% wool, 33% acrylic, 12% cashmere sportweight (4ply) yarn, 1¾oz (50g) balls, approx 137yd (125m) per ball:
   1 x ball each of shade 067 Sienna (orange) (C), shade 065 Clotted Cream (off white) (D), shade 089 Sapphire (blue), 092 Orange, 078 Lipstick Pink (pink), 099 Sea Green (green), 059 Mallard (dark blue) (E)

US size H/8 (5mm) and US size E/4 (3.5mm) crochet hooks

12mm black safety eyes

Yarn sewing needle

Gauge
Approx 15 sts x 11 rows over a 4in (10cm) square using US size H/8 (5mm) hook, half double crochet, and Cashmerino Aran.

Size
Adult

Finished measurements
Approx 21in (53.5cm) circumference, 8in (20cm) high

Abbreviations
approx approximately
beg begin(ning)
ch chain
dc double crochet
hdc half double crochet
rep repeat
RS right side
sc single crochet
sc2tog single crochet 2 stitches together
ss slip stitch
st(s) stitch(es)
tr treble
WS wrong side

Hat
Work in rounds on RS, placing st marker at beg of each round.
Round 1: Using MC and US size H/8 (5mm) hook, make 2ch, 8hdc in second ch from hook. *(8 sts)*
Round 2: 2hdc in each st to end. *(16 sts)*
Round 3: *1hdc in next st, 2hdc in next st; rep from * to end. *(24 sts)*
Round 4: *1hdc in each of next 2 sts, 2hdc in next st; rep from * to end. *(32 sts)*
Round 5: *1hdc in each of next 3 sts, 2hdc in next st; rep from * to end. *(40 sts)*
Round 6: *1hdc in each of next 4 sts, 2hdc in next st; rep from * to end. *(48 sts)*
Round 7: *1hdc in each of next 5 sts, 2hdc in next st; rep from * to end. *(56 sts)*
Round 8: *1hdc in each of next 6 sts, 2hdc in next st; rep from * to end. *(64 sts)*
Round 9: *1hdc in each of next 7 sts, 2hdc in next st; rep from * to end. *(72 sts)*
Rounds 10–21: 1hdc in each st to end. *(72 sts)*
Round 22: 1sc in each st to end.
Do not fasten off.
Insert first st marker here to denote back of hat.

First earflap:

1sc in each of next 6 sts. Do not turn.

Beg working in rows, turning at end of each row.

Row 1 (RS): 1sc in each of next 18 sts. Turn. *(18 sts)*

Row 2 (WS): 1ch, sc2tog, 1sc in each of next 14 sts, sc2tog. *(16 sts)*

Row 3: 1ch, 1sc in each st to end. *(16 sts)*

Row 4: 1ch, sc2tog, 1sc in each of next 12 sts, sc2tog. *(14 sts)*

Row 5: 1ch, 1sc in each st to end. *(14 sts)*

Row 6: 1ch, sc2tog, 1sc in each of next 10 sts, sc2tog. *(12 sts)*

Row 7: 1ch, 1sc in each st to end. *(12 sts)*

Row 8: 1ch, sc2tog, 1sc in each of next 8 sts, sc2tog. *(10 sts)*

Row 9: 1ch, 1sc in each st to end. *(10 sts)*

Row 10: 1ch, sc2tog, 1sc in each of next 6 sts. *(8 sts)*

Row 11: 1ch, 1sc in each st to end. *(8 sts)*

Row 12: 1ch, sc2tog, 1sc in next 4 sts, sc2tog. *(6 sts)*

Row 13: 1ch, 1sc in each st to end. *(6 sts)*

Row 14: 1ch, sc2tog, 1sc in each of next 2 sts, sc2tog. *(4 sts)*

Row 15: 1ch, 1sc in each st to end. *(4 sts)*

Row 16: 1ch, sc2tog (twice). *(2 sts)*

Row 17: 1ch, 1sc in each st to end. *(2 sts)*

Row 18: 1ch, sc2tog.

Second earflap:

With RS facing, join MC in next st along from end of Row 1 of First earflap.

1ch, 1sc in same st, 1sc in each of next 11st, place second st marker here to denote front of Hat, 1sc in each of next 12 sts. Do not turn. *(24 sts)*

Work in rows, turning at end of each row.

Row 1: 1sc in each of next 18 sts. Turn.

Rep Rows 2–18 of First earflap.

Edging:

With RS of work facing, join A at back of hat at start of straight edge in next st along after First earflap.

1ch, 1sc in same st, 1sc in each of next 11 sts along back of Hat to start of Second earflap, make 18 sc evenly down first edge of first Earflap.

3sc in bottom edge, make 18 sc evenly along other edge of Earflap, 1sc in each of next 24 sts along front of Hat, make 18 sc evenly along first edge of next Earflap; rep from ** to **, join with a ss in first sc. *(113 sts)*

Fasten off.

Leg and foot
(make 2)

Using US size H/8 (5mm) hook, on RS of hat join B in center st of 3 sts on edge of one Earflap, make 37ch.

Toe 1: 1sc in second ch from hook, 1sc in each of next 7 ch.

Toe 2: 9ch, 1sc in second ch from hook, 1sc in each of next 7 ch, ss in base of Toe 1.

Toe 3: 9ch, 1sc in second ch from hook, 1sc in each of next 7 ch.

Ss in base of Toe 1 to form foot.

1sc in each ch along leg back to Earflap, join with a ss in same place as joining st.

Fasten off.

Rep on other Earflap to make second Leg and Foot.

Top beak

Work in rounds, placing st marker at beg of each round.

Using C and US size E/4 (3.5mm) hook, make 2ch, 3sc in second ch from hook.

Round 1: 2sc in each st. *(6 sts)*

Round 2: 1hdc in each of next 4 sts, 1sc in next 2 sts. *(6 sts)*

Round 3: *1hdc in next st, 2hdc in next st; rep from * once more, 2sc in next st, 1sc in next st. (*9 sts*)

Round 4: *1hdc in each of next 2 sts, 2hdc in next st; rep once more, 1sc in each of last 3 sts. (*11 sts*)

Round 5: *1hdc in each of next 3 sts, 2hdc in next st; rep from * once more, 1sc in each of last 3 sts. (*13 sts*)

Round 6: *1hdc in each of next 4 sts, 2hdc in next st; rep from * once more, 1sc in each of last 3 sts. (*15 sts*)

Round 7: 1hdc in each st to end. (*15 sts*)

Ss in next st.

Fasten off, leaving long tail for sewing up.

Sew in tail end from starting point and turn right side out (this Top beak should have a slight curve, which is top of beak).

Sew opening together using long tail. Do not cut tail, this is used later for sewing onto Hat.

Bottom beak

Work in rounds, placing st marker at beg of each round.

Using C and US size E/4 (3.5mm) hook, make 2ch, 3sc in second ch from hook.

Round 1: 2sc in each st. (*6 sts*)

Round 2: *1hdc in next st, 2hdc in next st; rep from * once more, 1hdc in each of last 2 sts. (*8 sts*)

Round 3: *1hdc in each of next 2 sts, 2hdc in next st; rep from * once more, 1hdc in each of last 2 sts. (*10 sts*)

Round 4: *1hdc in each of next 3 sts, 2hdc in next st; rep from * once more, 1hdc in each of last 2 sts. (*12 sts*)

Round 5: *1hdc in each of next 4 sts, 2hdc in next st; rep from * once more, 2hdc in next st, 1hdc in last st. (*15 sts*)

Round 6: 1hdc in each st to end. (*15 sts*)

Ss in next st.

Fasten off, leaving long tail for sewing up.

Sew in tail end from starting point and turn RS out.

Sew opening together using long tail.

Sew Top beak to Bottom beak at straight edges (edges that have been sewn up).

Eyes

(*make 2*)

Work in rounds, placing st marker at beg of each round.

Using D and US size E/4 (3.5mm) hook, and leaving a long end of approx 6in (15cm), make 2ch, make 5sc into second ch from hook, join with ss to form a ring.

Round 1: 1ch, 1sc in next st, 2sc in each of next 4 sts, join with a ss in first sc. (*9 sts*)

Round 2: 1ch, 1sc in each st to end, join with a ss in first sc. (*9 sts*)

Round 3: 1ch, skip first st, sc2tog around, join with a ss in first sc.

Fasten off leaving a long tail.

Sew in ends but do not cut tails.

Turn eye RS out. Insert safety eyes into center of eye.

Use one of yarn tails to stuff center of eye and other tail to sew onto Hat approx 9 rows from bottom edge and 7 sts apart.

Comb

Work in rows, turning at end of each row.

Row 1: Using A and US size E/4 (3.5mm) hook, make 44ch leaving a long tail at beg, 1sc in second ch from hook, 1sc in each ch to end. Turn. *(43 sts)*

Row 2: 1ch, 1sc in first st, *skip 2 sts, 5dc in next st, skip 2 sts, 1sc in next st; rep from * to end.

Row 3: 1ch, 1sc in first st, *1hdc in next st, 2dc in next st, 5tr in next st, 2dc in next st, 1hdc in next st, 1sc in next st; rep from * to end.

Row 4: 1ch, 1sc in first st, *1sc in each of next 3 sts, 1hdc in next st, 2dc in next st, 5tr in next st, 2dc in next st, 1hdc in next st, 1sc in each of next 4 sts; rep from * to end.
Fasten off.

Insert a st marker at front edge of hat as a guide for sewing on comb, eyes and beak.
Center Comb on top of Hat, running from front of Hat to back (not side to side). Pin and sew on using long tail.
Center and sew Beak onto front edge of Hat, approx 1 row above edge.

Wattles

(make 2)

Worked from bottom edge (Row 1) to top edge (Row 13). Work in rows, turning at end of each row.

Using A and US size E/4 (3.5mm) hook, make 3ch,

Row 1: 2sc in second ch from hook, 2sc in last st. Turn. *(4 sts)*

Row 2: 1ch, 2sc in first st, 1sc in each of next 2 sts, 2sc in last st. *(6 sts)*

Row 3: 1ch, 1sc in each st to end. *(6 sts)*

Row 4: 1ch, 2sc in first st, 1sc in each of next 4 sts, 2sc in last st. *(8 sts)*

Row 5: 1ch, 1sc in each st to end. *(8 sts)*

Row 6: 1ch, 2sc in first st, 1sc in each of next 6 sts, 2sc in last st. *(10 sts)*

Rows 7–10: 1ch, 1sc in each st to end. *(10 sts)*

Row 11: 1ch, sc2tog over first two sts, 1sc in each of next 6 sts, sc2tog over last 2 sts. *(8 sts)*

Row 12: 1ch, 1sc in each st to end. *(8 sts)*

Row 13: 1ch, sc2tog, 1sc in each of next 4 sts, sc2tog. *(6 sts)*
Fasten off leaving a long tail for sewing on.

Sew straight edges of Wattles together.
Center straight edge of Wattle onto underside of bottom beak from back to front, then sew straight edge of Wattle along beak.
Sew approx 1in (2.5cm) of Wattles onto hat from top to bottom, along edge that is nearest to Hat.

Tail feathers

(make 5, 1 each color)

Using E and US size E/4 (3.5mm) hook, make 20ch, 1sc in second ch from hook and in each of next 2 ch, 1hdc in each of next 3 ch, 1dc in each of next 3 ch, 1tr in each of next 10 ch. *(19 sts)*
4ch, 1sc in same ch as last tr, 4ch.
Working on underside of ch that have just been worked into:
1tr in each of next 10 ch, 1dc in each of next 3 ch, 1hdc in each of next 3 ch, 1sc in each of last 3 ch (making last sc in tip of feather).
Fasten off.

With RS together, center one Tail feather at bottom edge at back of Hat and sew onto hat along bottom edge of feather. Place next two Tail feathers at an angle to fan out on top of central feather and sew in place. Place last two Tail feathers RS facing down between first and second feather and second and third feather, sew in place along bottom edge of feathers.

Mark the lizard

This is so cool, and it's also really good fun to make. Definitely for the die-hard reptile fan in your life!

Materials

Debbie Bliss Cashmerino Aran, 55% merino wool, 33% acrylic, 12% cashmere worsted (aran) yarn, 1¾oz (50g) balls, approx 98yd (90m) per ball:
    2 x balls of shade 065 Bark (greeny-brown) (MC)
    1 x ball of shade 027 Stone (pale gray) (A)

Louisa Harding Cassia, 75% wool, 25% nylon light worsted (DK) yarn, 1¾oz (50g) balls, approx 145yd (133m) per ball:
    1 x ball of shade 108 (lime) (B)

US size H/8 (5mm) and US size E/4 (3.5mm) crochet hooks

12mm brown safety eyes

Yarn sewing needle

Gauge

15 sts x 11 rows over a 4in (10cm) square using US size H/8 (5mm) hook, half double crochet, and Cashmerino Aran.

Size

Adult

Finished measurements

Approx 21in (53.5cm) circumference, approx 8in (20cm) high

Abbreviations

approx approximately
beg begin(ning)
ch chain
hdc half double crochet
hdc2tog half double crochet 2 stitches together
hdc3tog half double crochet 3 stitches together
rep repeat
RS right side
sc single crochet
ss slip stitch
st(s) stitch(es)
WS wrong side

Hat

Work in rounds on RS, placing st marker at beg of each round.

Round 1: Using MC and US size H/8 (5mm) hook, 2ch, 4hdc in second ch from hook. (4 sts)

Round 2: 2hdc in each st to end. (8 sts)

Round 3: Rep Round 2. (16 sts)

Round 4: *1hdc in next st, 2hdc in next st; rep from * to end. (24 sts)

Round 5: *1hdc in each of next 2 sts, 2hdc in next st; rep from * to end. (32 sts)

Round 6: *1hdc in each of next 3 sts, 2hdc in next st; rep from * to end. (40 sts)

Round 7: *1hdc in each of next 4 sts, 2hdc in next st; rep from * to end. (48 sts)

Round 8: *1hdc in each of next 5 sts, 2hdc in next st; rep from * to end. (56 sts)

Round 9: *1hdc in each of next 6 sts, 2hdc in next st; rep from * to end. (64 sts)

Round 10: *1hdc in each of next 7 sts, 2hdc in next st; rep from * to end. (72 sts)

Round 11: *1hdc in each of next 8 sts, 2hdc in next st; rep from * to end. (80 sts)

Rounds 12–23: 1hdc in each st to end. (80 sts)

Round 24: 1sc in each st to end. (80 sts)

Do not fasten off.

Tail:

Beg working in rows, turning at end of each row.

Row 1: 2ch (does not count as st throughout), 1hdc in each of next 25 sts. Turn.

Row 2: 2ch, 1hdc in each st to end. (25 sts)

Row 3: 2ch, hdc2tog, 1hdc in each of next 21 sts, hdc2tog. (23 sts)

Row 4: Rep Row 2. (23 sts)

Row 5: 2ch, hdc2tog, 1hdc in each of next 19 sts, hdc2tog. (21 sts)

Row 6: Rep Row 2. (21 sts)

Row 7: 2ch, hdc2tog, 1hdc in each of next 17 sts, hdc2tog. (19 sts)

Row 8: Rep Row 2. (19 sts)

Row 9: 2ch, hdc2tog, 1hdc in each of next 15 sts, hdc2tog. (17 sts)

Row 10: Rep Row 2. (17 sts)

Row 11: 2ch, hdc2tog, 1hdc in each of next 13 sts, hdc2tog. (15 sts)

Row 12: Rep Row 2. (15 sts)

Row 13: 2ch, hdc2tog, 1hdc in each of next 11 sts, hdc2tog. (13 sts)

Row 14: Rep Row 2. (13 sts)

Row 15: 2ch, hdc2tog, 1hdc in each of next 9 sts, hdc2tog. (11 sts)

Row 16: Rep Row 2. (11 sts)

Row 17: 2ch, hdc2tog, 1hdc in each of next 7 sts, hdc2tog. (9 sts)

Row 18: Rep Row 2. (9 sts)

Row 19: 2ch, hdc2tog, 1hdc in each of next 5 sts, hdc2tog. (7 sts)

Row 20: Rep Row 2. (7 sts)

Row 21: 2ch, hdc2tog, 1hdc in each of next 3 sts, hdc2tog. (5 sts)

Row 22: Rep Row 2. (5 sts)

Row 23: 2ch, hdc2tog, 1hdc in next st, hdc2tog. (3 sts)

Row 24: Hdc3tog.

Fasten off.

Spines

(make 11)

Work in rounds, placing st marker at beg of each round.

Round 1: Using A and US size H/8 (5mm) hook, 2ch, 4sc in second ch from hook. *(4 sts)*

Round 2: 2sc in each st to end. *(8 sts)*

Round 3: *1sc in each of next 3 sts, 2sc in next st; rep from * to end. *(10 sts)*

Round 4: *1sc in each of next 4 sts, 2sc in next st; rep from * to end. *(12 sts)*

Round 5: *1sc in each of next 5 sts, 2sc in next st; rep from * to end. *(14 sts)*

Round 6: *1sc in each of next 6 sts, 2sc in next st; rep from * to end. *(16 sts)*

Round 7: *1sc in each of next 7 sts, 2sc in next st; rep from * to end. *(18 sts)*

Round 8: *1sc in each of next 8 sts, 2sc in next st; rep from * to end. *(20 sts)*

Ss in next st.

Fasten off leaving a long tail for sewing on.

Press each Spine flat. Using long tail of yarn, sew spines in a row from center front of Hat to tip of Tail, using long tail.

Edging

With RS facing, join B in tip of Tail. Make 44sc evenly along edge of Tail until you reach edge of Hat. Make 1sc in each st around Hat. Make 44sc evenly along second edge of Tail until end. Make 1sc in tip of tail. Join with a ss in first sc. Fasten off.

Eyes

(make 2)

Work in rounds on RS, placing st marker at beg of each round.

Round 1: Using B and US size E/4 (3.5mm) hook, 2ch, 6sc in second ch from hook. *(6 sts)*

Round 2: 2sc in each st to end. *(12 sts)*

Round 3: *1sc in next st, 2sc in next st; rep from * to end. *(18 sts)*

Round 4: *1sc in each of next 2 sts, 2sc in next st; rep from * to end. *(24 sts)*

Round 5: *1sc in each of next 3 sts, 2sc in next st; rep from * to end. *(30 sts)*

Round 6: *1sc in each of next 4 sts, 2sc in next st; rep from * to end. *(36 sts)*

Round 7: *1sc in each of next 5 sts, 2sc in next st; rep from * to end. *(40 sts)*

Rounds 8–10: 1sc in each st to end. *(40 sts)*

Ss in next st.

Fasten off leaving a long tail.

Sew in end that has been left from first ch. Insert safety eye into center on RS of work.

Stuff lightly and sew eye onto side of Hat approx 5 rows from bottom edge and 7 to 8 stitches in from Front spines.

Who can resist these gorgeous loving eyes and floppy ears?

Poppy the labrador retriever

Materials
Debbie Bliss Rialto Chunky, 100% merino wool bulky (chunky) yarn, 1¾oz (50g) balls, approx 66yd (60m) per ball:
  3 x balls of shade 07 Gold (yellow) (MC)

Small amount of black bulky (chunky) yarn (A)

US size H/8 (5mm) crochet hook

Small amount of polyester toy stuffing

Yarn sewing needle

Gauge
Approx 14 sts x 10 rows over a 4in (10cm) square using US size H/8 (5mm) hook, half double crochet, and Rialto Chunky.

Size
Adult

Finished measurements
Approx 21in (53.5cm) circumference, 8in (20cm) high

Abbreviations
approx approximately
beg begin(ning)
ch chain
hdc half double crochet
rep repeat
RS right side
sc2tog single crochet 2 stitches together
sc single crochet
ss slip stitch
st(s) stitch(es)
WS wrong side

Hat
Work in rounds on RS, placing st marker at beg of each round.
Round 1: Using MC and US size H/8 (5mm) hook, make 2ch, 8hdc in second ch from hook. (8 sts)
Round 2: 2hdc in each st to end. (16 sts)
Round 3: *1hdc in next st, 2hdc in next st; rep from * to end. (24 sts)
Round 4: *1hdc in each of next 2 sts, 2hdc in next st; rep from * to end. (32 sts)
Round 5: *1hdc in each of next 3 sts, 2hdc in next st; rep from * to end. (40 sts)
Round 6: *1hdc in each of next 4 sts, 2hdc in next st; rep from * to end. (48 sts)
Round 7: *1hdc in each of next 5 sts, 2hdc in next st; rep from * to end. (56 sts)
Round 8: *1hdc in each of next 6 sts, 2hdc in next st; rep from * to end. (64 sts)
Rounds 9–21: 1hdc in each st to end. (64 sts)
Round 22: 1sc in each st to end.
Cut yarn, do not fasten off.
Place first st marker here to denote center back of Hat.

First earflap:
1sc in each of next 5 sts. Do not turn.
Beg working in rows, turning at end of each following row.
Row 1 (RS): 1sc in each of next 15 sts. Turn. (15 sts)
Row 2 (WS): 1ch (does not count as st throughout), sc2tog, 1sc in each of next 11 sts, sc2tog. (13 sts)
Row 3: 1ch, 1sc in each st to end. (13 sts)
Row 4: 1ch, sc2tog, 1sc in each of next 9 sts, sc2tog. (11 sts)
Row 5: 1ch, 1sc in each st to end. (11 sts)
Row 6: 1ch, sc2tog, 1sc in each of next 7 sts, sc2tog. (9 sts)
Row 7: 1ch, 1sc in each st to end. (9 sts)
Row 8: 1ch, sc2tog, 1sc in each of next 5 sts, sc2tog. (7 sts)
Row 9: 1ch, 1sc in each st to end. (7 sts)
Row 10: 1ch, sc2tog, 1sc in each of next 3 sts, sc2tog. (5 sts)
Rows 11–16: 1ch, 1sc in each st to end. (5 sts)
Do not fasten off.

Back of paw:

Row 17: 1ch, 2sc in first st, 1sc in each of next 3 sts, 2sc in last st. *(7 sts)*

Row 18: 1ch, 2sc in first st, 1sc in each of next 5 sts, 2sc in last st. *(9 sts)*

Rows 19–21: 1ch, 1sc in each st to end. *(9 sts)*

Row 22: 1ch, sc2tog, 1sc in each of next 5 sts, sc2tog. *(7 sts)*

Row 23: 1ch, sc2tog, 1sc in each of next 3 sts, sc2tog. *(5 sts)*

Row 24: 1ch, sc2tog, 1sc in next st, sc2tog. *(3 sts)*

Do not fasten off.

Front of paw:

Row 25: 1ch, 1sc in each st to end. *(3 sts)*

Row 26: 1ch, 2sc in first st, 1sc in next st, 2sc in next st. *(5 sts)*

Row 27: 1ch, 2sc in first st, 1sc in each of next 3 sts, 2sc in next st. *(7 sts)*

Row 28: 1ch, 2sc in first st, 1sc in each of next 5 sts, 2sc in next st. *(9 sts)*

Rows 29–31: 1ch, 1sc in each st to end. *(9 sts)*

Row 32: 1ch, sc2tog, 1sc in each of next 5 sts, sc2tog. *(7 sts)*

Row 34: 1ch, sc2tog, 1sc in each of next 3 sts, sc2tog. *(5 sts)*

Row 35: 1ch, 1sc in each st to end. *(5 sts)*

Fasten off leaving a long tail for sewing up Paw.

Second earflap:

With RS facing, join MC in next st along from end of Row 1 of First earflap.

1ch, 1sc in same st, 1sc in each of next 11 sts, place second st marker here to denote center front of hat, 1sc in each of next 12 sts. Do not turn. *(24 sts)*

Work in rows, turning at end of each following row.

Row 1: 1sc in each of next 15 sts. Turn.

Rep Rows 2–35 from First earflap to end of Front Paw.

Fold bottom Paws to WS of top Paws and sew all round using long tail.

Using A, embroider two claws in straight stitch (see page 18) on each Paw, using the photo as a guide.

Muzzle

Work in rounds, placing st marker at beg of each round.

Round 1: Using MC, make 2ch, 6sc in second ch from hook. *(6 sts)*

Round 2: 2sc in each st to end. *(12 sts)*

Round 3: *1sc in next st, 2sc in next st; rep from * to end. *(18 sts)*

Round 4: *1sc in each of next 2 sts, 2sc in next st; rep from * to end. *(24 sts)*

Round 5: *1sc in each of next 3 sts, 2sc in next st; rep from * to end. *(30 sts)*

Round 6: *1sc in each of next 4 sts, 2sc in next st; rep from * to end. *(36 sts)*

Rounds 7–11: 1sc in each st to end. *(36 sts)*

Ss in next st.

Fasten off leaving a long tail for sewing on.

Center Muzzle approx one row up from bottom edge. Leave small gap before stuffing lightly. Continue to close gap and sew in end. Using A, embroider nose in satin stitch (see page 18) and mouth in straight stitch (see page 18), using the photo as a guide.

Using A, embroider eyes in satin stitch (see page 18) approx 11 rows from bottom edge and 10 sts apart.

Ears

(make 2)

Row 1: Using MC, 3ch, 2sc in second ch from hook, 2sc in last ch. *(4 sts)*

Row 2: 1ch, 2sc in first st, 1sc in each of next 2 sts, 2sc in last st. *(6 sts)*

Row 3: 1ch, 1sc in each st to end. *(6 sts)*

Row 4: 1ch, 2sc in first st, 1sc in each of next 4 sts, 2sc in last st. *(8 sts)*

Row 5: 1ch, 1sc in each st to end. *(8 sts)*

Row 6: 1ch, 2sc in first st, 1sc in each of next 6 sts, 2sc in last st. *(10 sts)*

Row 7: 1ch, 1sc in each st to end. *(10 sts)*

Row 8: 1ch, 2sc in first st, 1sc in each of next 8 sts, 2sc in last st. *(12 sts)*

Rows 9–12: 1ch, 1sc in each st to end. *(12 sts)*

Row 13: 1ch, sc2tog over first 2 sts, 1sc in each of next 8 sts, sc2tog over last 2 sts. *(10 sts)*

Rows 14–21: 1ch, 1sc in each st to end. *(10 sts)*

Row 22: 1ch, sc2tog, 1sc in each of next 6 sts, sc2tog. *(8 sts)*

Row 23: 1ch, 1sc in each st to end. *(8 sts)*

Row 24: 1ch, sc2tog, 1sc in each of next 4 sts, sc2tog. *(6 sts)*

Fasten off leaving a long tail for sewing Ear to Hat.

Press Ears flat.

Sew Ears by placing upside down with RS of Ear on RS of Hat and sewing in straight line between Rows 22–23 of Ear and along the edge onto Hat, approx 3in (8cm) apart. Ear should then flop down. Place one stitch at bottom of ear to secure Ear down.

Sew in ends.

Often talked of as a spiritual animal, the wolf makes the perfect hat if you want to show your soulful side. It's made to fit a small adult head, but if you want to make it bigger just add more rounds on the increase rows and then increase the distance between earflaps by the amount of increases made.

Mister wolf

Materials
Debbie Bliss Lara, 58% merino wool, 42% superfine alpaca bulky (super chunky) yarn, 3½oz (100g) balls, approx 65yd (60m) per ball:
  1 x ball of shade 04 Yuri (light gray) (MC)
  1 x ball of shade 01 Pasha (off white) (A)
  1 x ball of shade 09 (Nadia) (black/white) (B)

Small amount of black bulky (chunky) yarn (C)

US size L/11 (8mm) and US size H/8 (5mm) crochet hooks

Small amount of polyester toy stuffing

Yarn sewing needle

Gauge
7 sts x 5½ rows over a 4in (10cm) square using US size L/11 (8mm) hook, half double crochet, and Debbie Bliss Lara.

Size
Adult

Finished measurements
Approx 21in (53.5cm) circumference, 8in (20cm) high

Abbreviations
approx approximately
beg begin(ning)
ch chain
hdc half double crochet
rep repeat
RS right side
sc single crochet
ss slip stitch
st(s) stitch(es)

Special abbreviation
5dcCL (5-double crochet cluster): *yoh, insert hook in next st, yoh, pull yarn through, yoh, pull through 2 loops, rep from * 4 times more, yoh, pull yarn through all 6 loops on hook.

Hat
Work in rounds, placing st marker at beg of each round.
Round 1 (RS): Using MC and US size L/11 (8mm) hook, 6ch, join with ss to form a ring.
Round 2: 2ch (counts as first hdc), 11hdc in ring, join with ss in top of first 2ch. (12 sts)
Round 3: 2ch (counts as first hdc), 1hdc in same st, 2hdc in each st to end, join with ss in top of first 2-ch. (24 sts)
Round 4: 2ch (counts as first hdc), 1hdc in same st, *1hdc in next st, 2hdc in next st; rep from * to last st, 1hdc in last st, join with ss in top of first 2-ch. (36 sts)
Rounds 5–8: 2ch (counts as first hdc), 1hdc in each st to end. (36 sts) Do not fasten off.

Earflap 1:
Work in rows, turning at ends of each row, using single crochet. Insert st marker.
Row 1 (RS): 1ch (does not count as st throughout), 1sc in first st, 1sc in each of next 7 sts. Turn. (8 sts)
Row 2: 1ch, sc2tog, 1sc in each of next of next 4 sts, sc2tog. (6 sts)

Row 3: 1ch, 1sc in each st to end. (6 sts)
Row 4: 1ch, sc2tog, 1sc in each of next 2 sts, sc2tog. (4 sts)
Row 5: 1ch, 1sc in each st to end. (4 sts)
Row 6: 1ch, [sc2tog] twice. (2 sts)
Row 7: 1ch, 1sc in each of next 2 sts. (2 sts)
Row 8: 1ch, sc2tog.
Fasten off.

Earflap 2:
With RS facing, join MC in ninth st along from end of Row 1 of First earflap.
Row 1: 1ch, 1sc in same st, 1sc in each of next 7 sts. Turn. (8 sts)
Row 2: 1ch, sc2tog, 1sc in each of next of next 4 sts, sc2tog. (6 sts)
Row 3: 1ch, 1sc in each st to end. (6 sts)
Row 4: 1ch, sc2tog, 1sc in each of next 2 sts, sc2tog. (4 sts)
Row 5: 1ch, 1sc in each st to end. (4 sts)
Row 6: 1ch, [sc2tog] twice. (2 sts)
Row 7: 1ch, 1sc in each of next 2 sts. (2 sts)
Row 8: 1ch, sc2tog.
Fasten off.

Edging:

With RS facing, using A, join yarn in last st made on Earflap 2, make 16ch, 5dcCL in second ch from hook, 1sc in next ch and each of next 13 ch to end of earflap, make 9sc evenly along side of earflap edge to Hat edge (back of Hat), make 1sc in each of next 9 sts to next earflap.

Make 8sc evenly along first side of earflap, 1sc in end st (tip of Earflap), make 16ch, 5dcCL in second ch from hook, 1sc in each of next 14 ch to end of earflap, make 9sc evenly along side of earflap edge to Hat edge (front of Hat), make 1sc in each of next 12 sts to next earflap. Make 9sc along side of earflap to end.

Join with ss in first sc.

Fasten off.

Muzzle

Using A and US size L/11 (8mm) hook, make 4ch, join with a ss to form a ring

Round 1: 1ch, 8sc in ring, join with ss in first sc.

Round 2: 1ch, 1sc in first st, 2sc in next st, *1sc in next st, 2sc in next st; rep from * to end, join with ss in first sc. *(12 sts)*

Rounds 3–4: 1ch, 1sc in each st, join with ss in first sc.

Round 5: 1ch, *1sc in each of next 3 sts, 2sc in next st; rep from * to end. *(15 sts)*

Fasten off.

Using small amount of black bulky (chunky) yarn, embroider nose in satin stitch (see page 18) and mouth in straight stitch (see page 18) onto Muzzle, using the photo as
a guide.

Stuff Muzzle lightly and sew onto front of Hat at the bottom edge.

Ears
(make 2)

Round 1: Using B and US size H/8 (5mm) hook, 2ch, 4sc in second ch from hook. *(4 sts)*

Round 2: 2sc in each st to end. *(8 sts)*

Round 3: *1sc in each of next 3 sts, 2sc in next st; rep from * once more. *(10 sts)*

Round 4: *1sc in each of next 4 sts, 2sc in next st; rep from * once more. *(12 sts)*

Round 5: *1sc in each of next 5 sts, 2sc in next st; rep from * once more. *(14 sts)*

Round 6: 1sc in each st to end.

Ss in next st.

Fasten off leaving a long tail for sewing on.

Place ears to the side of the head, pin and sew.

Eyes

Using small amount of C, embroider eyes using French knots (see page 19) approx 5 sts apart, using the photo as a guide.

Adam the fox

Great for cold days, this cheeky little fox takes no time at all to make. He's nocturnal, so wear him out at night too!

Materials

Debbie Bliss Cashmerino Aran, 55% merino wool, 33% acrylic, 12% cashmere worsted (aran) yarn, 1¾oz (50g) balls, approx 98yd (90m) per ball:

- 2 x balls of shade 048 Burnt Orange (orange) (MC)
- 1 x ball of shade 025 White (A)
- 1 x ball of shade 300 Black (B)

Small amount of black bulky (chunky) yarn (C)

US size H/8 (5mm) and US size E/4 (3.5mm) crochet hooks

Yarn sewing needle

Gauge

Approx 15 sts x 11 rows over a 4in (10cm) square using US size H/8 (5mm) hook, half double crochet, and Cashmerino Aran.

Size

Adult

Finished measurements

Approx 21in (53.5cm) circumference, 8in (20cm) high

Abbreviations

approx approximately
beg begin(ning)
ch chain
hdc half double crochet
rep repeat
RS right side
sc single crochet
ss slip stitch
st(s) stitch(es)
WS wrong side

Hat

Work in rounds on RS, placing st marker at beg of each round.
Round 1: Using MC and US size H/8 (5mm) hook, make 2ch, 8hdc in second ch from hook. *(4 sts)*
Round 2: 2hdc in each st to end. *(16 sts)*
Round 3: *1hdc in next st, 2hdc in next st; rep from * to end. *(24 sts)*
Round 4: *1hdc in each of next 2 sts, 2hdc in next st; rep from * to end. *(32 sts)*
Round 5: *1hdc in each of next 3 sts, 2hdc in next st; rep from * to end. *(40 sts)*
Round 6: *1hdc in each of next 4 sts, 2hdc in next st; rep from * to end. *(48 sts)*
Round 7: *1hdc in each of next 5 sts, 2hdc in next st; rep from * to end. *(56 sts)*
Round 8: *1hdc in each of next 6 sts, 2hdc in next st; rep from * to end. *(64 sts)*
Round 9: *1hdc in each of next 7 sts, 2hdc in next st; rep from * to end. *(72 sts)*
Rounds 10–19: 1hdc in each st to end. *(72 sts)*
Cut yarn, do not fasten off.
Round 20: Join A, 1hdc in each st to end. *(72 sts)*
Rounds 21–24: 1hdc in each st to end. *(72 sts)*
Round 25: Using B, 1sc in each st to end, ss in last st.
Fasten off.

Inner ear

(make 2)
Row 1: Using B and US size E/4 (3.5mm) hook, 2ch, 3sc in second ch from hook. *(3 sts)*
Row 2: 1ch, 2sc in first st, 1sc in next st, 2sc in last st. *(5 sts)*
Cut yarn, do not fasten off.
Row 3: Join A, 1ch, 1sc in each st to end. *(5 sts)*
Row 4: 1ch, 2sc in first st, 1sc in each of next 3 sts, 2sc in last st. *(7 sts)*
Row 5: 1ch, 1sc in each st to end. *(7 sts)*
Row 6: 1ch, 2sc in first st, 1sc in each of next 5 sts, 2sc in last st. *(9 sts)*
Row 7: 1ch, 2sc in first st, 1sc in each of next 7 sts, 2sc in last st. *(11 sts)*
Row 8: 1ch, 1sc in each st to end. *(11 sts)*
Row 9: 1ch, 2sc in first st, 1sc in each of next 9 sts, 2sc in last st. *(13 sts)*
Rows 10–11: 1ch, 1sc in each st to end. *(13 sts)*
Fasten off.

Outer ears

(make 2)
Row 1: Using B and US size E/4 (3.5mm) hook, 2ch, 3sc in second ch from hook. *(3 sts)*
Row 2: 1ch, 2sc in first st, 1sc in next st, 2sc in last st. *(5 sts)*
Cut yarn, do not fasten off.
Row 3: Join MC, 1ch, 1sc in each st to end. *(5 sts)*
Rows 4–11: Rep Rows 4–11 of Inner ear.
Fasten off.

Sew in ends.
Pin Inner and Outer ears WS together. Using MC and US size E/4 (3.5mm) hook, with RS facing and working through both pieces, sc around three edges, using C around Rows 1–2 at top end of Ears and making 3sc in each tip.
Fasten off leaving a long tail.

Sew Ears onto Hat with Ears curved slightly forward, and Inner ears facing to front.

Nose

Work in rounds, placing st marker at beg of each round.
Round 1: Using B and US size E/4 (3.5mm) hook, make 2ch, 6sc in second ch from hook. *(6 sts)*
Round 2: 2sc in each st to end. *(12 sts)*
Round 3: *1sc in next st, 2sc in next st; rep from * to end. *(18 sts)*
Round 4: *1sc in each of next 2 sts, 2sc in next st; rep from * to end. *(24 sts)*
Round 5: 1sc in each st to end. *(24 sts)*
Cut yarn, do not fasten off.
Round 6: Join MC, *1sc in each of next 3 sts, 2sc in next st; rep from * to end. *(30 sts)*
Rounds 7–14: 1sc in each st to end. *(30 sts)*
Ss in next st.
Fasten off leaving a long tail for joining.

Sew in ends.
Flatten nose and use long tail to sew open edge together.
With nose flat, center on front of Hat and sew edge to last row of MC.

Eyes

Using C, embroider eyes in satin stitch (see page 18) approx 5 rows up from last row of MC, using the photo as a guide.

I once looked after a goat for a while. He ate through the Internet cable and the Christmas lights, and did the usual goat-thing and jumped every gate or fence he was enclosed in.

Philip the goat

Materials

Debbie Bliss Cashmerino Aran, 55% merino wool, 33% acrylic, 12% cashmere worsted (aran) yarn, 1¾oz (50g) balls, approx 98yd (90m) per ball:
  2 x balls of shade 101 Ecru (off white) (MC)
  1 x ball of shade 066 Mustard (light brown) (B)

Debbie Bliss Rialto DK, 100% merino wool light worsted (DK) yarn, 1¾oz (50g) balls, approx 115yd (105m) per ball:
  1 x ball of shade 064 Mauve (pink) (A)

US size H/8 (5mm) and US size E/4 (3.5mm) crochet hooks

Yarn sewing needle

9mm black safety eyes

Small amount of polyester toy stuffing

Gauge

Approx 15 sts x 11 rows over a 4in (10cm) square using US size H/8 (5mm) hook, half double crochet, and Cashmerino Aran.

Size

Adult

Finished measurements

Approx 21in (53.5cm) circumference, 8in (20cm) high

Abbreviations

approx approximately
beg begin(ning)
ch chain
hdc half double crochet
rep repeat
RS right side
sc single crochet
sc2tog single crochet 2 stitches together
ss slip stitch
st(s) stitch(es)
WS wrong side

Hat

Work in rounds on RS, placing st marker at beg of each round.
Round 1: Using MC and US size H/8 (5mm) hook, make 2ch, 8hdc in second ch from hook. (8 sts)
Round 2: 2hdc in each st to end. (16 sts)
Round 3: *1hdc in next st, 2hdc in next st; rep from * to end. (24 sts)
Round 4: *1hdc in each of next 2 sts, 2hdc in next st; rep from * to end. (32 sts)
Round 5: *1hdc in each of next 3 sts, 2hdc in next st; rep from * to end. (40 sts)
Round 6: *1hdc in each of next 4 sts, 2hdc in next st; rep from * to end. (48 sts)
Round 7: *1hdc in each of next 5 sts, 2hdc in next st; rep from * to end. (56 sts)
Round 8: *1hdc in each of next 6 sts, 2hdc in next st; rep from * to end. (64 sts)
Round 9: *1hdc in each of next 7 sts, 2hdc in next st; rep from * to end. (72 sts)
Rounds 10–21: 1hdc in each st to end. (72 sts)
Round 22: 1sc in each st to end.
Do not fasten off.
Insert first st marker here to denote center back of hat.

First earflap:

1sc in each of next 6 sts. Do not turn.
Beg working in rows, turning at end of each row.
Row 1(RS): 1sc in each of next 18 sts. Turn. (18 sts)
Do not fasten off.
Row 2 (WS): 1ch (does not count as st throughout), sc2tog,1sc in each of next 14 sts, sc2tog. (16 sts)
Row 3: 1ch, 1sc in each st to end. (16 sts)
Row 4: 1ch, sc2tog, 1sc in each of next 12 sts, sc2tog. (14 sts)
Row 5: 1ch, 1sc in each st to end. (14 sts)
Row 6: 1ch, sc2tog, 1sc in each of next 10 sts, sc2tog. (12 sts)
Row 7: 1ch, 1sc in each st to end. (12 sts)
Row 8: 1ch, sc2tog, 1sc in each of next 8 sts, sc2tog. (10 sts)
Row 9: 1ch, 1sc in each st to end. (10 sts)
Row 10: 1ch, sc2tog, 1sc in each of next 6 sts, sc2tog. (8 sts)
Row 11: 1ch, 1sc in each st to end. (8 sts)
Row 12: 1ch, sc2tog, 1sc in next 4 sts, sc2tog. (6 sts)
Row 13: 1ch, 1sc in each st to end. (6 sts)
Row 14: 1ch, sc2tog, 1sc in each of next 2 sts, sc2tog. (4 sts)
Row 15: 1ch, 1sc in each st to end. (4 sts)
Row 16: 1ch, [sc2tog] twice. (2 sts)
Row 17: 1ch, 1sc in each st to end. (2 sts)
Row 18: 1ch, sc2tog.

Second earflap:
With RS facing, join MC in next st along from end of Row 1 of First earflap.

1ch, 1sc in same st, 1sc in each of next 11 sts, place second st marker here to denote center front of hat, 1sc in each of next 12 sts. Do not turn. (*24 sts*)

Work in rows, turning at end of each row.

Row 1: 1sc in each of next 18 sts. Turn.

Rep Rows 2–18 of First earflap.

Edging:
With RS of work facing, join MC at back of hat at start of straight edge in next st along after First earflap.

1ch, 1sc in same st, 1sc in each of next 11 sts along back of Hat to start of Second earflap.

Make 18sc evenly down first edge of First earflap.

3sc in bottom st of Earflap, Make 18sc evenly along other edge of Earflap, 1sc in each of next 24 sts along front of Hat, make 18sc evenly along first edge of next Earflap; rep from ** to **, join with a ss in first sc. (*114 sts*)

Fasten off.

Muzzle

Work in rounds, placing st marker to denote beg of each round.

Round 1: Using MC and US size E/4 (3.5mm) hook, make 2ch, 6sc in second ch from hook. (*6 sts*)

Round 2: 2sc in each st to end. (*12 sts*)

Round 3: *1sc in next st, 2sc in next st; rep from * to end. (*18 sts*)

Round 4: *1sc in each of next 2 sts, 2sc in next st; rep from * to end. (*24 sts*)

Round 5: *1sc in each of next 3 sts, 2sc in next st; rep from * to end. (*30 sts*)

Round 6: *1sc in each of next 4 sts, 2sc in next st; rep from * to end. (*36 sts*)

Rounds 8–12: 1sc in each st to end. (*36 sts*)

Ss in next st. Fasten off.

Nose

Work in rows, turning at end of each row.

Row 1: Using A and US size E/4 (3.5mm) hook, make 2ch, 3sc in second ch from hook. Turn. (*3 sts*)

Row 2: 1ch (does not count as st throughout), 2sc in first st, 1sc in next st, 2sc in last st. (*5 sts*)

Row 3: 1ch, 1sc in each st to end. (*5 sts*)

Row 4: 1ch, 2sc in first st, 1sc in each of next 3 sts, 2sc in last st. (*7 sts*)

Row 5: 1ch, 1sc in each st to end. (*7 sts*)

Row 6: 1ch, 2sc in first st, 1sc in each of next 5 sts, 2sc in last st. (*9 sts*)

Row 7: 1ch, 1sc in each st to end. *(9 sts)*
Fasten off, leaving a long tail for sewing onto Muzzle.

Stuff Muzzle lightly and sew onto Front of Hat at bottom edge and using A, embroider the mouth in straight stitch (see page 18), using the photo as guide.
Sew Nose onto Muzzle.

Eyes
(make 2)
Work in rounds, placing st marker at beg of each round.
Using MC and US size E/4 (3.5mm) hook, and leaving a long end of approx 6in (15cm), make 2ch, make 6sc into second ch from hook.
Round 1 (RS): 1ch (does not count as st throughout), 1sc in first st, 2sc in each of next 5 sts, join with ss in first sc. *(11 sts)*
Round 2: 1ch, 1sc in each st to end, join with ss in first sc. *(11 sts)*
Round 3: 1ch, skip first st, sc2tog around, join with ss in first sc.
Fasten off leaving a long tail.

Sew in ends but do not cut tails.
Keeping Eyes RS out, insert safety eye into center of each Eye.
Use one of yarn tails to stuff center of Eye and other other tail to sew onto Hat approx twelve rows up from bottom edge and twelve sts apart.

Outer ear
(make 2)
Work in rows, turning at end of each row.
Row 1: Using MC and US size E/4 (3.5mm) hook, make 2ch, 3sc in second ch from hook. Turn. *(3 sts)*
Row 2: 1ch (does not count as st), 2sc in first st, 1sc in next st, 2sc in last st. *(5 sts)*
Row 3: 1ch, 1sc in each st to end. *(5 sts)*
Row 4: 1ch, 2sc in first st, 1sc in each of next 3 sts, 2sc in last st. *(7 sts)*
Row 5: 1ch, 1sc in each st to end. *(7 sts)*
Row 6: 1ch, 2sc in first st, 1sc in each of next 5 sts, 2sc in last st. *(9 sts)*
Row 7: 1ch, 1sc in each st to end. *(9 sts)*
Row 8: 1ch, 2sc in first st, 1sc in each of next 7 sts, 2sc in last st. *(11 sts)*
Row 9: 1ch, 1sc in each st to end. *(11 sts)*
Rows 10–20: 1ch, 1sc in each st to end. *(11 sts)*
Fasten off, leaving a long tail for sewing Inner ear to Outer ear.

Inner ear
(make 2)
Using A, rep Rows 1–20 of Outer ear.
Press all ear pieces.

With RS together, pin and sew outside edges of Inner ear and Outer ear together leaving bottom edge open. Turn RS out.
Position ears on top of hat, approx 5½in (14cm) apart at top starting 6 rows down from top. Shape outer edges of ears towards middle, and pin and sew in place.

Horns
(make two)
Working on RS throughout.
Round 1: Using B and US size E/4 (3.5mm) hook, 2ch, 6sc in second ch from hook. *(6 sts)*
Round 2: 2sc in each st. *(12 sts)*
Round 3: *1sc in each of next 2 sts, 2sc in next st; rep from * to end. *(16 sts)*
Round 4: 1sc in each st to end. *(16 sts)*
Round 5: *1sc in each of next 2 sts, sc2tog; rep from * to end. *(12 sts)*
Cut yarn, do not fasten off.
Rounds 6–9: Join MC, 1sc in each st to end. *(9 sts)*
Ss in next st, fasten off.

Sew each Horn in between ears and top of Hat.

Beard
Cut approx 6 strands of MC, each approx 4in (10cm) in length.
Using a US size E/4 (3.5mm) hook, thread strands individually to make tassels at center bottom of Muzzle. Trim to length required.

Using MC, make two small pompoms (see page 17) and attach one to each end of Earflap.

One of my best friends is from Adelaide in Australia, and he always sends me photos of koala bears when he's visiting home. One of my first toys was a stuffed koala that my grandmother brought me back from Australia, so I have a lot of affection for them. Enjoy making the fluffy ears and be sure to make the nose an oval shape when stuffing.

Kym the koala

Materials

Debbie Bliss Cashmerino Aran, 55% merino wool, 33% acrylic, 12% cashmere worsted (aran) yarn, 1¾oz (50g) balls, approx 98yd (90m) per ball:
    2 x balls of shade 009 Grey (MC)
    1 x ball of shade 300 Black (B)

Debbie Bliss Angel, 76% mohair, 24% silk laceweight yarn, ⅞oz (25g) balls, approx 219yd (200m) per ball:
    1 x ball of 006 Ecru (off white) (A)

US size H/8 (5mm) and US size E/4 (3.5mm) crochet hooks

Yarn sewing needle

Gauge

Approx 15 sts x 11 rows over a 4in (10cm) square using US size H/8 (5mm) hook, half double crochet, and Cashmerino Aran.

Size

Adult

Finished measurements

Approx 21in (53.5cm) circumference, 8in (20cm) high

Abbreviations

approx approximately
beg begin(ning)
ch chain
dc double crochet
hdc half double crochet
rep repeat
RS right side
sc single crochet
sc2tog single crochet 2 stitches together
ss slip stitch
st(s) stitch(es)
WS wrong side

Hat

Work in rounds on RS, placing st marker at beg of each round.
Round 1: Using MC and US size H/8 (5mm) hook, make 2ch, 8hdc in second ch from hook. (8 sts)
Round 2: 2hdc in each st to end. (16 sts)
Round 3: *1hdc in next st, 2hdc in next st; rep from * to end. (24 sts)
Round 4: *1hdc in each of next 2 sts, 2hdc in next st; rep from * to end. (32 sts)
Round 5: *1hdc in each of next 3 sts, 2hdc in next st; rep from * to end. (40 sts)
Round 6: *1hdc in each of next 4 sts, 2hdc in next st; rep from * to end. (48 sts)
Round 7: *1hdc in each of next 5 sts, 2hdc in next st; rep from * to end. (56 sts)
Round 8: *1hdc in each of next 6 sts, 2hdc in next st; rep from * to end. (64 sts)
Round 9: *1hdc in each of next 7 sts, 2hdc in next st; rep from * to end. (72 sts)
Rounds 10–21: 1hdc in each st to end. (72 sts)

Round 22: 1sc in each st to end.
Do not fasten off.
Place first st marker here to denote center back of Hat.

First earflap:
1sc in each of next 6 sts. Do not turn.
Beg working in rows, turning at end of each row.
Row 1 (RS): 1sc in each of next 18 sts. Turn. (18 sts)
Do not fasten off.
Row 2 (WS): 1ch (does not count as st throughout), sc2tog, 1sc in each of next 14 sts, sc2tog. (16 sts)
Row 3: 1ch, 1sc in each st to end. (16 sts)
Row 4: 1ch, sc2tog, 1sc in each of next 12 sts, sc2tog. (14 sts)
Row 5: 1ch, 1sc in each st to end. (14 sts)
Row 6: 1ch, sc2tog, 1sc in each of next 10 sts, sc2tog. (12 sts)
Row 7: 1ch, 1sc in each st to end. (12 sts)
Row 8: 1ch, sc2tog, 1sc in each of next 8 sts, sc2tog. (10 sts)
Row 9: 1ch, 1sc in each st to end. (10 sts)
Row 10: 1ch, sc2tog, 1sc in each of next 6 sts, sc2tog. (8 sts)
Row 11: 1ch, 1sc in each st to end. (8 sts)

Row 12: 1ch, sc2tog, 1sc in next 4 sts, sc2tog. *(6 sts)*
Row 13: 1ch, 1sc in each st to end. *(6 sts)*
Row 14: 1ch, sc2tog, 1sc in each of next 2 sts, sc2tog. *(4 sts)*
Row 15: 1ch, 1sc in each st to end. *(4 sts)*
Row 16: 1ch, [sc2tog] twice. *(2 sts)*
Row 17: 1ch, 1sc in each st to end. *(2 sts)*
Row 18: 1ch, sc2tog.

Second earflap:
With RS facing, join MC in next st along from end of Row 1 of First earflap.
1ch, 1sc in same st, 1sc in each of next 11 sts, place second st marker here to denote center front of Hat, 1sc in each of next 12 sts. Do not turn. *(24 sts)*
Work in rows, turning at end of each row.
Row 1: 1sc in each of next 18 sts. Turn.
Rep Rows 2–18 of First earflap.

Edging:
With RS of work facing, join MC at back of hat at start of straight edge in next st along after First earflap.
1ch, 1sc in same st, 1sc in each of next 11 sts along back of Hat to start of Second earflap.
Make 18sc evenly down first edge of first Earflap.
3sc in bottom st of Earflap, make 18sc evenly along other edge of Earflap, 1sc in each of next 24 sts along front of Hat, make 18sc evenly along first edge of next Earflap; rep from ** to **, join with a ss in first sc. *(114 sts)*
Fasten off.

Ears

(make 4 pieces)
Work in rounds, placing st marker at beg of each round.
Round 1: Using MC and US size H/8 (5mm) hook, make 2ch, 6sc in second ch from hook. *(6 sts)*
Round 2: 2sc in each st to end. *(12 sts)*
Round 3: *1sc in first st, 2sc in next st; rep from * to end. *(18 sts)*
Round 4: *1sc in each of next 2 sts, 2sc in next st; rep from * to end. *(24 sts)*
Round 5: *1sc in each of next 3 sts, 2sc in next st; rep from * to end. *(30 sts)*
Round 6: *1sc in each of next 4 sts, 2sc in next st; rep from * to end. *(36 sts)*
Ss in next st, fasten off.

*Place two pieces WS together. Using MC and US size E/4 (3.5mm) hook join yarn in any st. Join pieces with sc seam (see page 17). Fasten off.

Using A and size US size H/8 (5mm) hook, join yarn in any st. 1ch, 1sc in same st, 2dc in same st, 3dc in each of next 20 sts, 1sc in next st. Fasten off leaving 14 sts unworked.

Rep from * for other Ear.

Keeping fluffy yarn at top, sew Ears in place on top of head, approx 3in (7.5cm) apart.

Nose

Work in rounds, placing st marker to denote beg of each round.

Round 1: Using B and US size E/4 (3.5mm) hook, make 12ch (foundation chain), 1hdc in second ch from hook, 1hdc in each of next 9 sts, 3hdc in last ch.

Working on underside of foundation chain, 1hdc in each of next 10-ch, 3hdc in first foundation chain. (26 sts)

Round 2: 1hdc in each of next 11 sts, 3hdc in next st (center stitch of 3-hdc from previous round), 1hdc in each of next 12 sts, 3hdc in next st (center stitch of 3-hdc), 1hdc in last st. (30 sts)

Rounds 3–4: 1hdc in each st to end. (30 sts)

Ss in next st, fasten off leaving a long tail for sewing on.

Lightly stuff the Nose with black yarn ends.

Place a st marker in bottom center edge of Nose.

Place Nose onto bottom edge of Hat, aligning center edge of Nose with center front of Hat. Sew Nose to Hat incorporating stuffing.

Using B, embroider eyes in satin stitch (see page 18), using the photo as a guide.

Tips

For the Nose, it's important to have the correct number of stitches at the end of the first round. Count stitches carefully.

In Round 2, the 3hdc are always made in the center stitch of the 3-hdc from the previous round. When working with a black yarn it can be difficult to see the stitches, so try putting a stitch marker in the second of the 3-hdc, which marks the center stitch.

suppliers

US Stockists

Knitting Fever
(Debbie Bliss yarns)
Stores nationwide
www.knittingfever.com

The Knitting Garden
(Debbie Bliss yarns)
www.theknittinggarden.org

Webs
(yarn, crochet hooks, accessories,
tuition)
75 Service Center Rd
Northampton, MA 01060
1-800-367-9327
www.yarn.com
customerservice@yarn.com

Wool2Dye4
(range of British yarns)
www.wool2dye4.com

Accessories
A.C. Moore
(crochet hooks, accessories)
Online and east coast stores
1-888-226-6673
www.acmoore.com

Hobby Lobby
(crochet hooks, accessories)
Online and stores nationwide
1-800-888-0321
www.hobbylobby.com

Jo-Ann Fabric and Craft Store
(crochet hooks, accessories)
Stores nationwide
1-888-739-4120
www.joann.com

Michaels
(crochet hooks, accessories)
Stores nationwide
1-800-642-4235
www.michaels.com

UK stockists

Craft bits
(safety eyes)
CPU Enterprises
1 Barncroft Villas
Manor House Street
Peterborough
PE1 2TL
01733 566617
www.craftbits.co.uk

Deramores
(yarn, crochet hooks, accessories)
0845 519 4573 or 01795 668144
www.deramores.com
customer.service@deramores.com

Designer Yarns
(distributor for Debbie Bliss yarns)
www.designeryarns.uk.com

Fyberspates Ltd
(yarn, crochet hooks)
01244 346653
www.fyberspates.co.uk
fyberspates@btinternet.com

Hobbycraft
(yarn, crochet hooks)
Stores nationwide
0330 026 1400
www.hobbycraft.co.uk

John Lewis
(yarn, crochet hooks, accessories)
Stores nationwide
03456 049049
www.johnlewis.com

Tuition
Nicki Trench
Crochet Club, workshops, accessories
www.nickitrench.com
nicki@nickitrench.com

Accessories
Addi Needles
(crochet hooks)
01529 240510
www.addineedles.co.uk
addineedles@yahoo.co.uk

index

acknowledgments

First of all I have to say thank you to all the animals I have ever known, and have yet to meet, who have inspired so many of these very cute hats!

I would like to say a big thank you to Cindy Richards for commissioning me, Anna Galkina for being her usual lovely, supporting self throughout the process, and also thanks to Penny Craig, Sally Powell, and the rest of the team at CICO Books for putting together such a lovely book. Thank you to the designer, Alison Fenton, and to the models, stylists, and photographer for doing such a great job, too.

A really big part of a crochet book such as this, with all the detailed patterns, is down to the checking and I'm really lucky to have the fabulous Jane Czaja as my pattern checker. I couldn't do this without her. She senses exactly just what is needed to put the patterns right, and is calm and reassuring throughout the process. Thanks also to Marie Clayton who, as always, has made an exceptional job of the editing.

I am forever grateful and appreciative of my super-great crocheter, Michelle Bull, for always pulling out the stops and patiently crocheting her way through the hats to help me reach my deadlines.

I'm very lucky to have access to some really beautiful yarns and, more than that, some really great suppliers. Special thanks to Graeme Knowles-Miller from Designer Yarns who is really quick at getting the yarns out and helpful when I couldn't find just the right colour. Also to Jeni Brown from Fyberspates for her gorgeous silk yarns.

As always when designing, I ask the opinion of my friends and family just in case I'm going way off the mark, so big thanks for love and support from my daughters, Camilla and Maddy, and thanks also to JK… for the inspiration for Mister Wolf and Jolyon the Polar Bear.